America!

I love her, so do you. We rejoice in the freedoms preserved for us here. We recognize God's guiding hand in the founding of the nation and in the safe-guarding of her liberties. Truly America is "a land choice above all other lands."

But inspired prophecies warn of future dangers if Americans fail to serve their God and keep his commandments.

This book is about preserving our freedoms. It proposes actions you can take to help maintain our liberties. It speaks of spiritual tasks, temporal deeds, essential attitudes, and using your personal influence for good. Read it, digest it, apply it, and touch others with its messages.

Duane S. Crowther

To Helen Mar,

to preserve your personal freedoms!

Deane S. Crowther

america

*God's
Chosen Land
of Liberty*

america

God's Chosen Land of Liberty

DUANE S. CROWTHER

ISBN: 0-88290-320-9
Library of Congress No.: 87-082115
Horizon Publishers Catalog & Order No.: 2007
First Printing, August 1987

Printed and distributed
in the United States of America by

Horizon
Publishers
& Distributors, Incorporated
50 South 500 West P.O. Box 490
Bountiful, Utah 84010-0490

Table of Contents

Table of Contents 7
Preface 9

Section I

The Freedoms of God's Promised Land

I.   **America: A Choice Land of Promise** 13
     Nephi's Vision of God's Guidance in America 14
     Statements by the Lehi Colony Concerning the Promised
     Land 16
     Jaredite Teachings Concerning the Land of Promise 17
     Latter-day Revelations Concerning America as a Land of
     Promise 18
     America Founded with Divine Assistance 19
     The U.S. Constitution Inspired of God 25
     Summary 40

II. **What's Right With America?**
     Freedom of Worship 43
     Freedom of Speech 43
     Freedom of the Press and News Media 44
     Freedom of Assembly 44
     Freedom to Petition for Governmental Redress 45
     Freedom to Bear Arms 45
     Freedom from Unlawful Quartering of Soldiers in
     Private Homes 45
     Freedom from Unreasonable Searches and Seizures 45
     Freedom from Imprisonment without Indictment 46
     Freedom from Double Jeopardy 46
     Freedom from Forced Confession 46
     Freedom from Punishment without Due Process
     of Law 46
     Freedom from Public Confiscation without
     Renumeration 46

Freedom from Improper Trials 46
Freedom from Excessive Bail 47
Freedom from Excessive Fines 47
Freedom from Cruel and Unusual Punishments 47
Freedom from Slavery or Involuntary Servitude 47
Freedom from State Laws Abridging Citizenship Rights . 48
Freedom to Vote 48
Freedom to Hold Public Office 48
Freedom to Own and Accumulate Property........... 48
Freedom of Information 49
Freedom of Communication 49
Freedom of Privacy 49
Freedom to Travel 50
Freedom to Choose Place of Residence 50
Freedom of Education 51
Freedom to Chooose Medical Care 51
Freedom from Want 51
Freedom of Vocational Choice 53
Freedom Through Economic Stability 53
Freedom Through Social Acceptance 54
Freedom of Family Life 54
Freedom Through Police Protection 55
Freedom of Artistic Expression 55
Freedom of Scientific Discovery 55
Freedom to Limit Government 55
Summary 56

Section II

Choosing a Course for the Future

III. Personal Preparation for the Last Days 61
    Adopt Attitudes Based on Gospel Principles 61
    Spiritual Preparations for Survival 69
    Temporal Preparations for Survival 93
    Interacting with Others in the Last Days Environment . 98
    In Conclusion.................................... 106
    Summary 107

List of Quotations 110

Preface

I love America! It is my home, my native land. It has been great and good—a bastion of freedom and liberty. America has enjoyed the blessings and guidance of God, and her people have been protected through divine providence.

I have partaken of the liberties which she has granted to her citizens—privileges which are denied to people in many other lands. These liberties I value highly, and I regard them as priceless gems to be preserved at all costs. In the shadow of her freedoms I work, I plan, I dream, I hope, I build for the future. I seek America's well-being, her progress and her protection, for my future is inseparably connected with hers. If she grows and prospers, I may progress also; if she endures trauma and agony, I also must suffer. I am an American citizen. Like every American—my future and fate is inextricably related to the future of this great country.

There are many ways in which a citizen may work for his country. He may be active in political affairs, or work for the accomplishment of social goals. He may seek to improve the environment, or pursue better law enforcement methods, or render service through youth groups. Almost always he will serve in those capacities which give outlet for his best talents and abilities. By doing so, he gives the best of himself and accomplishes the greatest good.

I am no different. I am an author and publisher by profession. I seek to use my best skills as an expression of my patriotism and love of country. *America—God's Chosen Land of Liberty* is my way of contributing something of worth towards the betterment of this great nation.

In this book I have endeavored to accomplish three objectives. First, I have sought to show from the scriptures that this is truly a chosen land established through the direction and ministrations of a kind and loving God. He guided those who came to it, directed those who wrote its great constitution, and preserves it as a land of liberty and an inheritance for his people, so long as its inhabitants will serve Him and live in righteousness upon it.

Second, I have attempted to list many of the freedoms which are so abundantly enjoyed by Americans. This land is recognized worldwide as a land of liberty, a nation with a glorious heritage and an inspiring history, and a country with potential for a glorious future. For more than two centuries it has been the symbol of hope and opportunity which has drawn immigrants from countless countries like a powerful magnet. The freedoms enjoyed by this nation's inhabitants should not be blindly accepted nor thoughtlessly taken for granted.

9

To help us ponder their boundless implications, I have enumerated many of them, adding a brief explanation concerning each of the freedoms listed.

There are many conditional prophecies found in the scriptures which warn of difficult times which lie ahead for the inhabitants of America. This is not a book about prophecy, nor a book about the cataclysmic events of the last days. The future of America, as seen in prophetic utterance concerning the last days, is treated in detail in another volume.[1]   But the third objective of this book is to recommend in depth improved actions on the course American Latter-day Saints should undertake for their personal future.

Recommendations are made concerning the adoption of attitudes based on gospel principles, the need for spiritual and temporal preparations for survival, and ways in which the Saints should interact with others in the last days environment. These suggestions for future personal and family conduct are essential and far-reaching. They deal with basic philosophies of life that are significant and profound. If practiced collectively by the millions of Church members scattered across the land, their implementation can do much to perserve our nation's freedoms in the perilous times which lie ahead.

It is my sincere desire that this book will touch many lives for good. I truly hope that it will strengthen testimonies of the divine origin of this great nation, that it will cause recommitment to the preservation of the many divinely inspired liberties we enjoy, and that it will give valuable guidance to many who are seeking a personal orientation for their conduct in the years to come.

I seek to bless others through new insights, and to help them bless themselves through righteous and decisive actions. And I seek to invoke the blessings of heaven upon this land by helping its citizens to so live that they merit those great blessings from above. May we so live as to retain that divine guidance and protection in the years to come.

Duane S. Crowther

---

1. See *Inspired Prophetic Warnings*. (Bountiful, Utah: Horizon Publishers & Distributors, Inc., 1987.)

The Freedoms of God's Promised Land

America: A Choice Land of Promise

I

An oft-cited principle in Latter-day Saint theology is that the Americas are a chosen land which God has designated and reserved for a righteous people. This belief has its origin in the Book of Mormon, which repeatedly refers to these continents as a land especially blessed by the Lord. That volume tells of several groups who were led to the Americas by the hand of God.

As early as the second chapter of the book, a revelation from the Lord to Nephi, the son of the prophet Lehi, is recorded:

> ...inasmuch as ye shall keep my commandments, ye shall prosper, and *shall be led to a land of promise; yea, even a land which I have prepared for you*; yea; a land which is *choice above all other lands.* [1]

While still in the Palestine area, Nephi was given instructions from the Holy Spirit, which caused him to comment on the expectations he held concerning the land of promise:

> *Behold the Lord slayeth the wicked to bring forth his righteous purposes.* It is better that one man should perish than that a nation should dwindle and perish in unbelief.
> And now, when I, Nephi, had heard these words, I remembered the words of the Lord which he spake unto me in the wilderness, saying that: *Inasmuch as thy seed shall keep my commandments, they shall propsper in the land of promise.* [2]

As Nephi was endeavoring to obtain a copy of the scriptures so that his people might have their sacred message, his father, Lehi, told his mother, Sariah, of the land of promise and rejoiced that they would be led there:

> . . .I know that I am a visionary man; for if I had not seen the thigs of God in a vision I should not have known the goodness of God, but had tarried at Jerusalem, and had perished with my brethren.
> *But behold, I have obtained a land of promise, in the which things I do rejoice;* [3]

---

1. 1 Ne. 2:20. Nephi received this message in a wilderness area near the Red Sea, about 600 B.C., as he and his family were fleeing from Jerusalem.
2. 1 Ne. 4:13-14.
3. 1 Ne. 5:4-5.

Attaining the choice land was an ever-present goal for the Lehi colony as they traveled.[1]

Nephi's Vision of God's Guidance in America

Even before crossing the ocean to arrive in the Americas, Nephi was given a glorious vision in which he was shown many events which would transpire in the promised land. He saw that Lehi's descendants would multiply and become multitudes of people,[2] that there would be wars among them,[3] and that they would build many cities.[4] He saw that the Lamb of God would come among them, that Christ would choose and ordain twelve disciples here in the Americas,[5] and that the Savior's coming would be preceded by great destruction.[6] Nephi was shown that righteousness would prevail until the fourth generation after the Savior's advent, and then wars would again break out.[7] He saw that the descendants of his brother Laman (the Lamanites, forefathers of the American Indians) would conquer his descendants,[8] and that the Lamanites would then war among themselves for many generations,[9] as they dwindled in unbelief.[10]

Nephi's vision swept forward to the end of the dark ages when he saw many "nations and kingdoms of the Gentiles"[11] which were across the seas from the Lamanites here in the Americas.[12] In his vision he foresaw what many Latter-day Saints believe to be the coming of Columbus to the Americas, and observed that his coming would be inspired by the Spirit of God:

> And I looked and beheld a man among the Gentiles, who was separated from the seed of my brethren by the many waters; and *I beheld the Spirit of God, that it came down and wrought upon the man; and he went forth upon the many waters,* even unto the seed of my brethren, who were in the promised land.[13]

---

1. See 1 Nephi 5:4-5.
2. 1 Ne. 12:1.
3. 1 Ne. 12:2.
4. 1 Ne. 13:3.
5. 1 Ne. 12:6-10.
6. 1 Ne. 12:4-5.
7. 1 Ne. 12:11-15.
8. 1 Ne. 12:19-20.
9. 1 Ne. 12:21.
10. 1 Ne. 12:22-23.
11. 1 Ne. 13:1-9.
12. 1 Ne. 13:10.
13. 1 Ne. 13:12.

Nephi was then shown in his vision that the Spirit of God would inspire other Gentiles to leave the captivity and oppression of their homelands and to sail to the Americas.[1] He described the coming of these early American settlers and emphasized that they were led by God:

> And *I beheld the Spirit of the Lord, that it was upon the Gentiles, and they did prosper and obtain the land for their inheritance;* and I beheld that they were white, and exceedingly fair and beautiful, like unto my people before they were slain.
>
> And it came to pass that I, Nephi, beheld that the Gentiles who had gone forth out of captivity did humble themselves before the Lord; and *the power of the Lord was with them.*[2]

In his vision, Nephi foresaw the revolutionary struggles of these settlers as they won independence for the Americas. He was shown that *"the wrath of God was upon all those that were gathered together against them to battle"* and that they "were *delivered by the power of God* out of the hands of all other nations."[3]

Nephi was aware of the religious attitudes which would be manifested among the people of the Americas, and foretold the influence which the Bible would have among them.[4] He was also shown that the inhabitants of America would be *"lifted up by the power of God above all nations,* upon the face of the land which is choice above all other lands."[5]

Although he was aware that there would be contention between the American settlers and the Indian inhabitants,[6] Nephi saw that the Lamanites would be preserved by God and that they would not be destroyed.[7]

And then, in his vision, Nephi was told that God, in his mercy, would bring forth his "plain and precious" gospel here in the Americas,[8] and that the gospel would come first to the "Gentile" settlers and then would be carried to the Lamanites, the descendants of Lehi.[9] Those who would seek to establish the Lord's "Zion" in

---

1. 1 Ne. 13:13.
2. 1 Ne. 13:15-16.
3. 1 Ne. 13:17-19.
4. 1 Ne. 13:20-29.
5. 1 Ne. 13:30.
6. 1 Ne. 13:14.
7. 1 Ne. 13:30-31.
8. 1 Ne. 13:34-35.
9. 1 Ne. 13:34-35.

that day would be blessed with "the gift and power of the Holy Ghost."[1]

Nephi's powerful vision continued into the future and details significant events which must yet come to pass. Every event in the prophetic timetable which he foresaw in this vision 600 years B.C. has come to pass so far. His inspired insight reveals repeatedly that God has guided and shaped the growth of America and that this is a choice land—a land of promise.

Statements by the Lehi Colony Concerning the Promised Land

When Lehi and his colony arrived in the Americas that great prophet bore witness of God's covenant concerning the land to which they had been led:

> ...we have obtained a land of promise, a land which is choice above all other lands; a land which the Lord God hath covenanted with me should be a land for the inheritance of my seed. Yea, the Lord hath covenanted this land unto me, and to my children forever, and also all those who should be led out of other countries by the hand of the Lord.
> Wherefore, I, Lehi, prophesy according to the workings of the Spirit which is in me, that there shall none come into this land save they shall be brought by the hand of the Lord.
> Wherefore, this land is consecrated unto him whom he shall bring.[2]

Lehi's son, the prophet Jacob, also spoke concerning the role of America as a promised land. He testified that

> ...this land, said God, shall be a land of thine inheritance, and the Gentiles shall be blessed upon the land.
> And this land shall be a land of liberty unto the Gentiles, and there shall be no kings upon the land, who shall raise up unto the Gentiles.[3]

Jacob reminded his followers that the Americas were consecrated by God as an inheritance for the descendants of Lehi.

---

1. 1 Ne. 13:37.
2. 2 Ne. 1:5-7. Lehi's statement is prophetic and continues into the future.
3. 2 Ne. 10:10-11. The Savior, as He visited the Americas, spoke of the coming of the Gentiles in the last days, and observed that "it is wisdom in the Father that they should be established in this land, and be set up as a free people by the power of the Father, that these things might come forth from them unto a remnant of your seed, that the covenant of the Father may be fulfilled which he hath covenanted with his people, O house of Israel;. . ." (3 Ne. 21.4)

He repeated the Lord's word that

> ...I will *consecrate this land unto thy seed,* and them who shall be numbered among thy seed, *forever,* for the land of their inheritance; for *it is a choice land, saith God unto me, above all other lands,* wherefore I will have all men that dwell thereon that they shall worship me, saith God.[1]

A later admonition by Jacob to his people included his reference to "this land, *which is a land of promise unto you and to your seed.*"[2]

It is clear, then, that early Book of Mormon prophets recognized that God had shaped their lives for good by bringing them to a land which was to receive His special blessings and protection.

Jaredite Teachings Concerning the Land of Promise

The people of an earlier migration to the Americas also were shown by revelation that their destination was a land which was special in the eyes of God. This group, the Jaredites, left the Middle East at the time of the Tower of Babel. Like the Lehi colony, they also crossed the ocean under divine direction to settle in a land of promise. The Lord told the Brother of Jared:

> ...I will go before thee into *a land which is choice above all the lands of the earth.*
> And there will I bless thee and thy seed, and raise up unto me of thy seed, and of the seed of thy brother, and they who shall go with thee, a great nation. And there shall be none greater than the nation which I will raise up unto me of thy seed, upon all the face of the earth. And thus I will do unto thee because this long time ye have cried unto me.[3]

As he wrote the Jaredite history, the prophet Moroni told of the Jaredite migration to the Americas and commented that

> ...The Lord would not suffer that they should stop beyond the sea in the wilderness, but he would that they should come forth even *unto the land of promise, which was choice above all other lands, which the Lord God had preserved for a righteous people.*[4]

---

1. 2 Ne. 10:19.
2. Jac. 2:12.
3. Eth. 1:42-43.
4. Eth. 2:7. This passage also continues to become an inspired prophetic warning which will be discussed later in this book.

Moroni reported a revelation from the Lord to the brother of Jared which the Master concluded with the statement that "these are my thoughts upon the land which I shall give you for your inheritance; for *it shall be a land choice above all other lands.*"[1]

The promised-land concept remained with the Jaredites throughout their history. Moroni commented on a group of them many centuries later, observing that

> ...never could be a people more blessed than were they, and more prospered by the hand of the Lord. And they were *in a land that was choice above all lands, for the Lord had spoken it.*[2]

The last of the Jaredite prophets, Ether, told his people

> ...of all things, from the beginning of man; and that after the waters had receded from off the face of this land *it became a choice land above all other lands, a chosen land of the Lord; wherefore the Lord would have that all men should serve him who dwell upon the face thereof;*
> And that it was *the place of the New Jerusalem,* which should come down out of heaven, and the holy sanctuary of the Lord.[3]

Latter-day Revelations Concerning America as a Land of Promise

The theme of America being under the special providence of God continued into revelations given since the restoration of the gospel and the Lord's Church.

In the summer of 1828, the Lord spoke to Joseph Smith concerning the faith and prayers of the Book of Mormon prophets.

---

1. Eth. 2:15.
2. Eth. 10:28.
3. Eth. 13:2-3. His prophecy continued to tell of a New Jerusalem, a city which is to be built in America in the last days:

   And that *a New Jerusalem should be built upon this land, unto the remnant of the seed of Joseph,* for which things there has been a type.
   For as Joseph brought his father down into the land of Egypt, even so he died there; wherefore, the Lord brought a remnant of the seed of Joseph out of the land of Jerusalem, that he might be merciful unto the seed of Joseph that they should perish not, even as he was merciful unto the father of Joseph that he should perish not.
   Wherefore, *the remnant of the house of Joseph shall be built upon this land; and it shall be a land of their inheritance;* and they shall build up a holy city unto the Lord, like unto the Jerusalem of old; and they shall no more be confounded, until the end come when the earth shall pass away. (Eth. 13:6-8.)

He told Joseph that

> ...their faith in their prayers was that this gospel should be made known also, if it were possible that other nations should possess this land;
>
> And *thus they did leave a blessing upon this land in their prayers, that whosoever should believe in this gospel in this land might have eternal life;*
>
> Yea, that it might *be free unto all of whatsoever nation, kindred, tongue, or people they may be.*[1]

A revelation on January 2, 1831, at a Church conference at Fayette, New York, again conveyed the Lord's promise that America would be a land of inheritance for the saints:

> And I hold forth and deign to give unto you greater riches, even *a land of promise,* a land flowing with milk and honey, upon which there shall be no curse when the Lord cometh;
>
> And *I will give it unto you for the land of your inheritance,* if you seek it with all your hearts.
>
> And this shall be *my covenant with you, ye shall have it for the land of your inheritance, and for the inheritance of your children forever,* while the earth shall stand, and ye shall possess it again in eternity, no more to pass away.
>
> But, verily I say unto you that in time ye shall have no king nor ruler, for I will be your king and watch over you.
>
> Wherefore, hear my voice and follow me, and *you shall be a free people,* and ye shall have no laws but my laws when I come, for I am your lawgiver, and what can stay my hand?[2]

America Founded with Divine Assistance

A frequent message of LDS General Authorities has been that the founding fathers of America functioned under divine guidance

---

1. D & C 10:49-51.
2. D & C 38:18-22. His promise was followed a few verses later with a warning:

   > Ye hear of wars in far countries, and you say that there will soon be great wars in far countries, but ye know not the hearts of men in your own land.
   >
   > I tell you these things because of your prayers; wherefore, treasure up wisdom in your bosoms, lest the wickedness of men reveal these things unto you by their wickedness, in a manner which shall speak in your ears with a voice louder than that which shall shake the earth; but if ye are prepared ye shall not fear.
   >
   > And that ye might escape the power of the enemy, and be gathered unto me a righteous people, without spot and blameless—
   > (D & C 38:29-31.)

as they established this nation and led it through the perils of its first century. Over the years, they have cited numerous examples in world and American history to show how God has shaped the destiny of America. Their comments, when taken collectively, serve to illustrate that this view is widely held by Church leadership.

Columbus, for instance, bore witness of having received aid from God as he made his memorable voyage. The following statement made by the discoverer of America was cited in a recent general conference by Elder Mark E. Petersen of the Council of the Twelve:

> The Lord was well disposed to my desire and he bestowed upon me courage and understanding; knowledge of seafaring he gave me in abundance,....and of geometry and astronomy likewise.... *The Lord with provident hand unlocked my mind, sent me upon the sea, and gave me fire for the deed.* Those who heard of my enterprise called it foolish, mocked me and laughed. *But who can doubt that the Holy Ghost inspired me?*[1]

William Penn, the founder of the city in which the Declaration of Independence was later signed, recognized the need for divine guidance when he warned that *"those people who are not governed by God will be ruled by tyrants."*[2]

George Washington, on several occasions, acknowledged God's hand in the guiding of this country toward liberty. Following the battle of Yorktown, during the Revolutionary War, he gave instructions that

> *Divine service is to be performed tomorrow* in the several brigades and divisions. The Commander-in-Chief earnestly recommends that the troops not on duty should universally attend with that seriousness of deportment and gratitude of heart which *the recognition of such reiterated and astonishing interposition of Providence* demands of us.[3]

In his farewell address to the army made November 2, 1782, Washington told how "the singular interpositions of Providence in our feeble condition were such as could scarcely escape the observ-

---

1. Jacob Wasserman, *Columbus, the Don Quixote of the Seas* (New Brunswick: Rutgers University Press, 1959), pp. 19-20, as quoted in *CR*, April, 1967, pp. 111. A statement by Columbus to King Ferdinand is cited from the same source: *"I came to your majesty as the emissary of the Holy Ghost."* (Wasserman, pp. 46.)
2. William Penn, as cited by Elder Richard L. Evans of the Council of the Twelve, "Our Legacy of Liberty," *IE*, Vol. 54, No. 9, Sept., 1951, p. 656.
3. As cited by Elder Mark E. Petersen of the Council of the Twelve, *CR*, April, 1967, p. 111.

ance of the most unobserving."[1] While speaking to Congress on April 30, 1789, Washington spoke of the belief Americans held that God had aided them:

> *No people can be bound to acknowledge and adore the invisible hand which conducts the affairs of men more than the people of the United States.* Every step by which they have advanced to the character of an independent nation seems to have been *distinguished by some token of Providential agency.*[2]

He then commented on the place of religion and morality in the nation, observing that

> Of all the dispositions and habits which lead to political prosperity, *religion and morality are indispensable supports....* Reason and experience both forbid us to expect that national morality can prevail in exclusion of religious principle.[3]

---

1. *Ibid.*, p. 112.
2. *Ibid.*, also cited by Elder Ezra Taft Benson of the Council of the Twelve, *CR*, April, 1952, p. 59.
3. Benson, *Ibid.*, p. 59. Elder Wendell J. Ashton, the General Secretary of the Deseret Sunday School Union, cited other interesting items about George Washington:

   To delve into the lives of these patriots reveals an abundance of strong religious conviction.... As a boy, George wrote his motto in his notebook: "Labor to keep alive in your breast that little spark of celestial fire, conscience." He was a regular attender at his church, taking an active part in his parishes at Alexandria and Pohick.

   But Washington's deep-rooted faith branched out beyond chapel walls. Winthrop, the historian, tells us, "It is an interesting tradition that, during the prayers with which Dr. Duche opened that meeting [the First Continental Congress] at Carpenter's Hall on September 5, 1774, while most of the delegates were standing, Washington was kneeling." [Robert C. Winthrop, *Presidents of the United States*, edited by J. G. Wilson, p. 19.]

   Washington's true humility shone out when Lewis Nicola, a colonel in his army, apprised him of a movement afoot, after the war, to make the general their king. "Banish these thoughts from your mind, and never communicate, from yourself or anyone else, a sentiment of a like nature," was the fiery reply. [*Ibid.*, p. 25.]

   Two days after he had received a proclamation from Congress announcing the cessation of hostilities with Britain, Washington ordered the army chaplains to "render thanks to Almighty God." [*Ibid.*, p. 27].

   Again, in his inaugural address, Washington's thought rose heavenward: "It would be peculiarly improper to omit in this first official act, my fervent supplication to that Almighty Being who rules over the universe, who presides in the councils of nations, and whose providential aids can supply every human defect." (The Signers of the Constitution," *IE*, Vol. 45, No. 9, Sept., 1942, pp. 563, 598.)

Patrick Henry's dramatic declaration at the Second Revolutionary Convention (Richmond, Virginia, March 23, 1775) was recalled by President David O. McKay:

> Is life so dear, or peace so sweet, as to be purchased at the price of chains and slavery? Forbid it, Almighty God! I know not what course others may take; but *as for me, give me liberty or give me death!* [1]

During the Constitutional Convention in 1787, a speech was made by **Benjamin Franklin** requesting that prayer be held. President J. Reuben Clark, Jr., cited it in a discourse illustrating the divinely-inspired nature of the U.S. Constitution:

> The small progress we have made after four or five weeks close attendance and continual reasonings with each other—our different sentiments on almost every question, several of the last producing as many noes as ays, is methinks a melancholy proof of the imperfection of the Human Understanding. We indeed seem to feel our own want of political wisdom, since we have been running about in search of it. We have gone back to ancient history for models of Government, and examined the different forms of those Republics which having been formed with the seeds of their own dissolution now no longer exist. And we have viewed Modern States all round Europe, but find none of their Constitutions suitable to our circumstances.
>
> In this situation of this Assembly, groping as it were in the dark to find political truth, and scarce able to distinguish it when presented to us, *how has it happened, Sir, that we have not hitherto once thought of humbly applying to the Father of lights to illuminate our understandings?* In the beginning of the Contest with G. Britain, *when we were sensible of danger we had daily prayer in this room for the divine protection.— Our prayers, Sir, were heard, and they were graciously answered. All of us who were engaged in the struggle must have observed frequent instances of a Superintending providence in our favor.* To that kind providence we owe this happy opportunity of consulting in peace on the means of establishing our future national felicity. *And have we now forgotten that powerful friend? or do we imagine that we no longer need his assistance?* I have lived, Sir, a long time, and the longer I live, the more convincing proofs I see of this truth—*that God governs in the affairs of men.* And if a sparrow cannot fall to the ground without his notice, is it probable that an empire can rise without his aid? We have been assured, Sir, in the sacred writings, that 'except the Lord build the House they labour in vain that build it.' I firmly believe this; and I also believe that without his concurring aid we shall succeed in this political building no better than the Builders of Babel: We shall be divided by our little partial local interest; our projects will be confounded, and we ourselves shall become a reproach and bye word down to future ages. And what is worse, mankind may hereafter from this

---

1. President David O. McKay, President of the Church, *CR*, October, 1961, p. 5

unfortunate instance, despair of establishing Governments by Human Wisdom and leave it to chance, war and conquest. [1]

Elder Delbert L. Stapley quoted a statement made by **Daniel Webster** in 1852 in which he urged America to be true to God:

> *If we and our posterity shall be true to the Christian religion; if we and they shall live always in the fear of God and shall respect his commandments;...we may have the highest hopes of the future fortunes of our country,* and we may be sure of one thing: Our country will go on prospering. But if we and our posterity reject religious instruction and authority, violate the rules of eternal justice, trifle with the unjunctions of morality, and recklessly destroy the political constitution which holds us together, *no one can tell how sudden a catastrophe may overwhelm us, that shall bury all our glory in profound obscurity.*
>
> Should that catastrophe happen let it have no history. Let the horrible narrative never be written. Let its fate be that of the lost books of Livy which no human eye shall ever read, or the missing Pleiad of which no man can ever know more than that it is lost, and lost forever. [2]

Statements by **Abraham Lincoln** have frequently been cited by LDS General Authorities to show that divine guidance has shaped this nation. Mr. Lincoln said,

> Unborn ages and visions of glory crowd upon my soul, the realization of all which, however, is in the hands and good pleasure of Almighty God; but, *under His divine blessing, it will be dependent on the character and the virtues of ourselves, and of our posterity.*
>
> And let me say, gentlemen, that *if we and our posterity shall be true to the Christian religion—if we and they shall live always in the fear of God, and shall respect His commandments—if we and they shall maintain just, moral sentiments, and such conscientious convictions of duty as shall control the heart and life—we may have the highest hopes of the future fortunes of our country,* and if we maintain those institutions of government and that political union, exceeding all praise as much as it exceeds all former examples of political associations, we may be sure of one thing—that, while our country furnishes materials for a thousand masters of historic art, it will afford no topic for a Gibbon. It will have no decline and fall. It will go on prospering and to prosper.
>
> *But if we and our posterity reject religious instruction and authority, violate the rules of eternal justice, trifle with the injunctions of morality,*

---

1. President J. Reuben Clark, Jr., of the First Presidency, *CR*, April, 1957, pp. 51-52.
2. Elder Delbert L. Stapley, of the Council of the Twelve, *CR*, October, 1963, pp. 112-113. Mr. Webster was speaking to the New York Historical Society on Feb. 22, 1852. (Also cited by Elder Mark E. Petersen, (*CR*, Oct. 1967, p. 68), and Elder Sterling W. Sill (*CR*, Oct., 1970, p. 78).

and recklessly destroy the political constitution which holds us together, no man can tell how sudden the catastrophe may overwhelm us, that shall bury all our glory in profound obscurity.[1]

When leaving for Washington after being elected President, Lincoln commented to his neighbors that

> *Without the assistance of that Divine Being I cannot succeed. With that assistance I cannot fail.* Trusting in him who can go with me and remain with you, and be everywhere for good, let us confidently hope that all may yet be well. To his care commending you, as I hope in your prayers you will commend me, I bid you an affectionate farewell.[2]

Another experience of Abraham Lincoln's, which followed the Battle of Gettysburg, was related by Elder Thorpe B. Isaacson:

> General Sickles had noticed that before the battle of Gettysburg, upon the result of which, perhaps, the fate of this nation hung, President Lincoln was apparently free from the oppressive care which frequently weighed him down. After it was all past, the general asked President Lincoln how it was that he felt so free from the oppressive care previously noticeable. He answered:
>
> 'Well, I will tell you how it was. In the pinch of your campaign up there, when everybody seemed panic-stricken and nobody could tell what was going to happen, oppressed by the gravity of affairs, I went to my room one day and I locked the door and *I got down on my knees before Almighty God and prayed to him mightily for victory at Gettysburg.* I told him this war was his war and our cause was his cause, but we could not stand another Fredericksburg or Chancellorsville. *Then and there I made a solemn vow to Almighty God that if he would stand by our boys at Gettysburg, I would stand by him.* After that, I don't know how it was, and I cannot explain it, but soon *a sweet comfort crept into my soul. The feeling that God had taken this whole business into his own hands and that things would go right at Gettysburg,* and that is why I had no fears about you.'[3]

These statements, each of them cited by LDS Church leaders, all demonstrate the Latter-day Saint belief that this nation was brought into existence and preserved under the guidance and direction of God. They are typical of many other quotations cited in the frequently-delivered discourses and sermons on patriotic themes given by LDS Church leaders.

---

1. *Petersen, op. cit., CR*, April, 1967, p. 112.
2. *Ibid.*
3. Elder Thorpe B. Isaacson, Assistant to the Twelve, *CR*, October, 1962, p. 29.

The U.S. Constitution Inspired of God

A revelation given to Joseph Smith on December 16, 1833, contains the clear assertion that the Constitution of the United States of America is an inspired document. In this revelation, the Lord refers to the

> ...constitution of the people, which I have suffered to be established, and should be maintained for the rights and protection of all flesh, according to just and holy principles;
>
> That every man may act in doctrine and principle pertaining to futurity, according to the moral agency which I have given unto him, that every man may be accountable for his own sins in the day of judgment.
>
> Therefore, it is not right that any man should be in bondage one to another.
>
> And for this purpose have I established the Constitution of this land, by the hands of wise men whom I raised up unto this very purpose, and redeemed the land by the shedding of blood.[1]

Four months earlier, the Lord had revealed the principle that the

> ...law of the land which is constitutional, supporting that principle of freedom in maintaining rights and privileges, belongs to all mankind, and is justifiable before me.
>
> Therefore, I, the Lord, justify you, and your brethren of my church, in befriending that law which is the constitutional law of the land;[2]

Hundreds of discourses or statements on the Constitution and its divine origin have been delivered by the brethren over the years, primarily based on these two passages. Certainly one of the most outstanding was the penetrating summary of the Constitution's history and message given by President J. Reuben Clark, Jr., in general conference on Saturday, April 6, 1957. He said, in part:

Organization of Constitutional Convention

The Constitution of the United States was framed in Independence Hall, Philadelphia, May 14, 1787, to September 17, 1787. The Framers

---

1. D & C 101:77-80. The Prophet Joseph Smith, in the dedicatory prayer for the Kirtland, Ohio Temple, beseeched the Lord, saying, "May those principles, which were so honorably and nobly defended, namely, the Constitution of our land, by our fathers, be established forever." (D & C 109:54)
2. D & C 98:5-6.

were delegates sent thereto by the Thirteen Colonies. Seventy-four were appointed; fifty-five reported at the Convention; nineteen did not attend; thirty-nine signed the Constitution. Representatives signed from each of the Colonies except Rhode Island.

Bill of Rights

The Constitution as signed lacked a Bill of Rights, though these rights were discussed in the Convention. As the Colonies voted to ratify the Constitution, each proposed amendments to remedy the omission. Over one hundred amendments were proposed. Some forty to fifty were eliminated as duplications. Seventeen were finally approved by the House of the First Congress; the Senate reduced the number to twelve, which were sent to the various legislatures for ratification. The final returns showed that ten had been ratified.

Historical Experience of Framers

The Framers and their fathers had in the preceding seventy-five years, fought through four purely European wars—in America between the British and her colonists on one side, and the French and her Indian allies on the other. The colonists had little, if any concern in the European issues. They fought because the homelands fought. In the first three of these wars the colonists lost much, suffered massacres. Yet at the end of each war, each European government returned, each to the other, the gains either had made in America. The colonists had heavy losses, had no gains except the experience that builded up over the decades, experience that aided them, first, in winning their independence, and, thereafter, in establishing this Government.

No wonder Washington in his Farewell Address counseled against foreign entanglements. He stated the reasons drawn from colonial experience.

The French and Indian War, the last of the four, broke the French foothold on the Continent. Washington participated in that war as an officer and suffered in Braddock's defeat at Fort Duquesne.

During a part of this whole period, the colonial legislatures had been fighting against royal representatives; in the earlier decade the fathers of the Framers carried on these contests; in the latter years, many of the Framers were themselves involved.

Movement for Independence

The movement for independence began soon after the close of the French and Indian War; for example, the Committees of Correspondence. Some of the very best minds and ablest men in the Colonies participated. Framers served on these earlier revolutionary bodies. Many Framers were members of the Continental Congress. When the Revolution came, they had the experiences, bitter as to both men and money, that came to that Congress in raising troops and materials of war. They had knowledge. Some were experienced in the actual problems of conducting a war. One at least, Franklin, had seen distinguished service in the diplomatic field and continued so to serve.

Characters of Framers

The Framers were men of affairs in their own right. Some were distinquished financiers. More than half of them were university men, some educated in the leading American colleges—Harvard, Yale, Columbia, Princeton, William and Mary; others in the great colleges of Great Britain—Oxford, Glasgow, Edinburgh. Washington and Franklin were amoung those who had no college education. Altogether there were seventy-four delegates appointed; fifty-five who reported at the Convention, "all of them" it has been said, "respectable for family and for personal qualities." Of these fifty-five, only thirty-nine were present at the signing. Nineteen failed to attend.

They were men of varied political beliefs. Some were Federalists; some anti-Federalists. Some seemed favorable to a mere revamping of the Articles of Confederation.

No Political "Blueprint" Available

The amazing thing is that there was not in all the world's history a government organization even among confederacies, that could be taken by the Framers as a preliminary blueprint for building the political structure they were to build. Franklin declared:

"We have gone back to ancient history for models of Government, and examined the different forms of those Republics which, having been formed with the seeds of their own dissolution, now no longer exist. And we have viewed Modern States all round Europe, but find none of their Constitutions suitable to our circumstances."

They had been in session for about a month (June 26, 1787) when Madison declared:

"...as it was more than probable we were now digesting a plan which in its operation would decide forever the fate of Republican Gov't we ought not only to provide every guard to liberty that its preservation could require, but be equally careful to supply the defects which our own experience had particularly pointed out."

Who the Framers Were

A little further detail about the thirty-nine Framers who actually signed the document will be useful.

Of those thirty-nine signers, twenty-six had seen service in the Continental Congress. They knew legislative processes and problems. Thirteen had served both the Continental Congress and in the Army. What a wealth of experience they had obtained in both legislative and executive duties. Of the nineteen who served as officers—they knew the problems of armed forces in the field; and of these seventeen, four had served on Washington's staff.

Let us go down the roll: Washington, the "Father of his Country," and Madison, sometimes called the "Father of the Constitution," were later Presidents of the United States. Hamilton (a financial genius) was Secretary of the Treasury under Washington. McHenry (Maryland) was Secretary of War under Washington. Randolph (Virginia) acted as Attorney General for Washington and later as his Secretary of State. Rutledge (South Carolina), a distinguished jurist, was later Chief Justice in the United States Supreme Court. Oliver Ellsworth (absent when the Constitution was signed) was also later a Chief Justice of the Supreme Court. Blair, Paterson, and Wilson were later Justices of the Supreme Court. (Wilson had been on the Board of War and Ordnance in the Second Continental Congress.)

Benjamin Franklin, a philosopher and scientist, had behind him years of most distinguished and successful diplomatic service. King (Massachusetts) was later a Senator and thereafter Minister to Great Britain. Charles Pinckney (South Carolina) was Minister to Spain. Dickinson (Delaware) founded Dickinson College, and Johnson (Connecticut) was President of Columbia College. Gerry (Massachusetts) was later Vice-President of the United States, and Ingersoll (Pennsylvania) a candidate for the Vice-Presidency.

Gorham (Massachusetts) and Mifflin (Pennsylvania) had been Presidents of the Continental Congress; Clymer (Pennsylvania), Continental Treasurer; Robert Morris (Pennsylvania), Superintendent of Finances; Sherman (Connecticut), a member of the Board of War and Ordnance, all in the Continental Congress.

We might add, as among the most distinguished of this group, the other Morris (Gouverneur) from Pennsylvania, and the other Pinckney (Charles Cotesworth) from South Carolina.

There were many other distinguished men. They were distinguished before the time of the Convention; they won great distinction after. Men of affairs and influence, they were in their respective Colonies, later States. They were all seasoned patriots of loftiest patriotism. They were not backwoods men from the far-off frontiers, not one of them.

What a group of men of surpassing abilities, attainments, experience, and achievements. *There has not been another group of men in all the one hundred seventy years of our history, no group that even challenged the supremacy of this group.* Gladstone solemnly declared:

"The American Constitution is the most wonderful work ever struck off at a given time by the brain and purpose of man."

After departing from the theme of his explanation to comment on the basic Doctrine and Covenants passages mentioned above, he continued:

These Framers of the Constitution were the men who the Lord "raised up unto this very purpose, and redeemed the land by the shedding of blood," making it ready for the blessings proclaimed for all.

Preparation of Framers

No more clearly does it appear that Moses was so trained in the royal Egyptian courts that he could lead ancient Israel out of bondage, or that Brother Brigham was so trained, in directing the exodus of the Saints from Missouri to Nauvoo, that he could lead modern Israel from the mobbings and persecutions of the East to the freedom of the mountain fastnesses of the West; neither one was more clearly trained for his work than these Framers were trained for theirs—rich in intellectual endowment and ripened in experience. They were equally as the others in God's hands; he guided them in their epochmaking deliberations in Independence Hall.

The Framers were deeply read in the facts of history; they were learned in the forms and practices and systems of the governments of the world, past and present; they were, in matters political, equally at home in Rome, in Athens, in Paris, and in London; they had a long, varied, and intense experience in the work of governing their various Colonies; they were among the leaders of a weak and poor people that had successfully fought a revolution against one of the great Powers of the earth; they were among them some of the ablest, most experienced and seasoned military leaders of the world.

As to all matters under consideration by the Convention, the history of the world was combed for applicable experiences and precedents.

The whole training and experiences of the colonists had been in the Common Law, with its freedoms and liberties even under their kings. They knew the functions of legislative, executive, and judicial arms of government.

Then he explained the basic principles of the Constitution and their importance:

Some Constitutional Principles

Time is not available now to consider in detail the work of the Convention nor the Constitution that was framed. A very few principles only, and they among the basic ones, may be mentioned. You all know them; they are now merely recalled to your minds. Sometimes we miss the import of them.

Three Independent Branches

First—The Constitution provided for three departments of government—the legislative, the executive, and the judicial.

These departments are mutually independent the one from the other.

Each department was endowed with all the powers and authority that the people through the Constitution conferred upon that branch of government—the legislative, the executive, and the judicial, respectively.

No Encroachment by One Branch upon Another

No branch of the government might encroach upon the powers conferred upon another branch of government. In order to forestall foreseeable encroachments, the Convention provided in the Constitution itself for a very few invasions by one or the other, into one of the departments, to make sure that one department should not absorb the functions of the other or encroach thereon, or gain an overbalancing power and authority against the other. These have been termed "checks and balances."

Non-delegation of Powers

A third principle that was inherent in all the provisions of the Constitution was that none of the departments could delegate its powers to others. The courts of the country have from the first insisted upon the operation of this principle. There have been some fancy near-approaches to such an attempted delegation, particularly in recent years, and some unique justifying reasoning therefor, but the courts have consistently insisted upon the basic principle, which is still operative.

An examination of the records of the Convention will show how anxiously earnest the Framers were to set up these and other principles of free government.

No Kings in America

The Convention seems to have experienced no really serious difficulty in setting up a judiciary department, nor in certain aspects, the legislative department with its powers, until it came to those powers which dealt with matters that in some governments had been regarded as belonging to the executive. You will recollect that practically all of these Framers had suffered under George III and his Minister, Lord North. So they abandoned the British model, for, as Randolph said, "...the fixt genius of the people of America required a different form of Government." This ruled out royalty.

It might be noted that Washington, as the Revolution closed, had definitely scotched at Newburgh, the kingship idea.

Kings and America

Of course, the Framers did not know (no living mortal then knew) that centuries before a prophet of the Lord had declared as to America:

"Behold, this is a choice land, and whatsoever nation shall possess it shall be free from bondage, and from captivity, and from all other nations under heaven, if they will but serve the God of the land, who is Jesus Christ, who hath been manifested by the things which we have written." (Ether 2:12.)

Nor did the Framers know (again, no living mortal then knew) that centuries after this prophecy, but still centuries before the Framers met, another prophet had declared:

"And this land shall be a land of liberty unto the Gentiles." (2 Nephi 10:11.)

The unhappy, short-lived experiences of the Dom Pedros in Brazil and of Maximilian in Mexico seem the exceptions that prove the rule. The Spirit of the Lord was leading.

The National Executive

In providing for the executive department, there was considerable discussion as to whether the executive department should be one person or several. Commenting upon a proposal for three, Randolph said their unity would be "as the foetus of monarchy."

Who should choose, elect, or appoint (the terms were used almost interchangeably) the Chief Executive was exhaustively debated; so was the problem of the length of his term, from one year, to Hamilton's during "good behaviour," including the question whether he should be ineligible for re-election, and whether he should be subject to impeachment.

Power to Declare War

But one of their most searching examinations related to the war powers of government, including the power to declare war. It became clear very early in the debates that as Chief Executive, the President should execute the laws passed by Congress. But he was also made Commander in Chief of the Army and Navy of the United States and of the State Militia when called into the service of the United States. The delegates were fearfully anxious over this function of government. There was one suggestion that the Commander in Chief should not personally go into the field with the troops, so fearful were they of his power.

Where War Powers Rest

But in whom should rest the so-called war powers? This was the urgent problem. It soon became clear that the Convention was unalterably opposed to endowing the President with these war powers; it was conceded he should have the power to repel invasions, but not to commence war, which meant he could not declare war.

Chief Executives Conceived as Plain Human Beings

Some of the arguments made in this connection, involving the possibility of a military usurper, remind one of the potential calamities pictured by Lincoln in his prophetic Lyceum Address, where he sketched what an ambitious, fame-and-power-seeking executive might do.

Various other potential actions by the executive were explored. Future Presidents of the Republic were conceived as including men capable of doing the things that ambitious men in power had done over the ages. Men were still human, had the same urges and ambitions. The earnest effort was to make as nearly impossible as could be, the malfeasances of the past by men in high executive office in the future; and seemingly perhaps beyond everything else as a practical matter, *to prevent the President from taking us into war of his own volition.* The Framers therefore provided that the war powers, including the declaration of war, should rest exclusively in the Congress, both by express provisions, and, as the record shows, by the conscious intent of the Framers.

The Net Position of the National Executive

The net result may be stated thus: as Chief Executive the President was to enforce the laws passed by Congress, including those passed by Congress in the exercise of the war powers that were explicitly and exclusively possessed by Congress; as Commander in Chief of the Army and Navy of the United States and of the Militia of the States when called into the actual service of the United States, he was to direct the military operations thereof in the field, with the powers incident thereto.

These principles should never be forgotten by any free, liberty-loving American, the kind of American the Constitution and the Bill of Rights make of us, and in which they were designed to protect us.

The People Are Sovereign

Furthermore, under our form of government, we the people of the United States, as the Preamble to the Constitution declares, formed this government. We alone are sovereign. We are wholly free to exercise our sovereign will in the way we prescribe. The sovereignty is not personal, as under the Civil Law. The Constitution expressly provides the only way in which we may change our Constitution.

We may well repeat again: We the people have all the powers we have not delegated away to our government, and the institutions of government have such powers and those only as we have given to them. The total residuum of powers, including all rights and liberties not given up by us to Federal or State Governments, is still in us, to remain so till we constitutionally provide otherwise. Under the Civil Law that basically governs Continental Europe, the people have only such rights as a personal sovereign or his equivalent bestows, the residuum remaining in him or them. Wherever and whenever powers are exercised by any person or branch of our government that are not granted by the Constitution, such powers are to that extent usurpations.

He then related the Constitution to the religion of the Latter-day Saints:

The Constitution and Ourselves

Will not each of you ask yourself this question: What would probably have happened if Joseph Smith had been born and had attempted to carry on his work of the Restoration of the Gospel and the Holy Priesthood, if he had been born and had sought to go forward in any other country in the world?

Must we go far to seek why God set up this people and their government, the only government on the face of the earth, since the Master was here, that God has formally declared was set up at the hands of men whom he raised up for that very purpose, and the fundamental principles of which he has expressly approved?

Constitution Is Part of My Religion

Having in mind what the Lord has said about the Constitution and its Framers, that the Constitution should be "established, and should be maintained for the rights and protection of all flesh," that it was for the protection of the moral agency, free agency, God gave us, that its "principle of freedom in maintaining rights and privileges, belongs to all mankind," all of which point to the destiny of the free government our Constitution provides, unless thrown away by the nations—having in mind all this, with its implications, speaking for myself, I declare that the divine sanction thus repeatedly given by the Lord himself to the Constitution of the United States as it came from the hands of the Framers with its coterminous Bill of Rights, makes of the principles of that document an integral part of my religious faith. It is a revelation from the Lord. I believe and reverence its God-inspired provisions. My faith, my knowledge, my testimony of the Restored gospel, based on the divine principle of continuous revelation, compel me so to believe.

Thus has the Lord approved of our political system, an approval, so far as I know, such as he has given to no other political system of any other people in the world since the time of Jesus.

The Constitution, as approved by the Lord, is still the same great vanguard of liberty and freedom in human government that it was the day it was written. No other human system of government, affording equal protection for human life, liberty, and the pursuit of happiness, has yet been devised or vouchsafed to man. Its great principles are as applicable, efficient, and sufficient to bring today the greatest good to the greatest number, as they were the day the Constitution was signed. Our Constitution and our Government under it, were designed by God as an instrumentality for righteousness through peace, *not war*.

Our Constitutional Destiny

Speaking of the destiny that the Lord has offered to mankind in his declaration regarding the scope and efficacy of the Constitution and its principles, we may note that already the Lord has moved upon many nations of the earth so to go forward. The Latin American countries have followed our lead and adopted our constitutional form of government, adapted to their legal concepts, without compulsion or restraint from us. Likewise, the people of Canada in the British North America Act have embodied great principles that are basic to our Constitution. The people of Australia have likewise followed along our governmental footpath. In Canada and in Australia, the great constitutional decisions of John Marshall and his associates are quoted in their courts and followed in their adjudications. I repeat, none of this has come because of force of arms. The Constitution will never reach its destiny through force. God's principles are taken by men because they are eternal and true, and touch the divine spirit in men. This is the only true way to permanent world peace, the aspiration of men since the beginning. God never planted his Spirit, his truth, in the hearts of men from the point of a bayonet.

The Framers had their dark days in their work. There were discouragements, there were hours of near hopelessness for some. Yet, as they were engaged in God's work, and he was at the helm, we know it was as certain as the day dawn, that Satan would be there also, with this thwarting design.

But I see in their divers views, their different concepts, even the promotion of their different local interests, not the confusion which challenged Franklin, but a searching, almost meticulous study and examination of the fundamental principles involved, and the final adoption of the wisest and best of it all—I see the winnowing of the wheat, the blowing away of the chaff.

After telling of the request for prayer by Benjamin Franklin,[1] President Clark bore his personal witness concerning the Constitution and the role the Saints must play in its preservation:

---

1. See pp. 22-23.

My Witness

Out of more years, but of far, far less wisdom and experience, I echo Franklin's testimony "that God governs in the affairs of men," and that without his concurring aid we shall build in vain, and "our projects will be confounded, and we ourselves shall become a reproach and bye word down to future ages."

I bear my testimony that without God's aid, we shall not preserve our political heritage neither to our own blessing, nor to the blessing of the downtrodden peoples of the world.

In broad outline, the Lord has declared through our Constitution his form for human government. Our own prophets have declared in our day the responsibility of the Elders of Zion in the preservation of the Constitution. We cannot, guiltless, escape that responsibility. We cannot be laggards, nor can we be deserters.

On the back of the chair in which Washington sat as President during the Convention, was carved a half-hidden sun, showing just above a range of hills. As the signing of the Constitution was about over, Franklin observed to some fellow delegates:

"I have often and often, in the course of the session, and the vicissitudes of my hopes and fears as to its issue, looked at that (sun) behind the President, without being able to tell whether it was rising or setting; but now, at length, I have the happiness to know that it is a rising, and not a setting sun."

Such was the prophecy that marked the closing of the greatest political convention of all time, for the Lord was there working out his purposes in a system he could endorse.

God give us the power, each of us, to enshrine in our hearts the eternal truths of our Constitution; that come what may, we shall never desert these truths, but work always and unceasingly that, as Lincoln said, "government of the people, by the people, for the people, shall not perish from the earth."

Such is my prayer, and I ask it in the name of Jesus. Amen.[1]

An *Improvement Era* article by Wendell J. Ashton, entitled "The Signers of the Constitution," in September, 1942, presented an excellent introduction to the Constitution. Elder Ashton presented the accompanying chart which gives information on each of these men (see next page). He then commented on many of the men, as follows:

That the framers of the Constitution formed an assemblage of great men no student of History can doubt. Three-fourths of the delegates had served in Congress. But in the Mormon way of thinking, these pillars of government were more than intellectual giants; they, in the words of Brigham Young, "were inspired from on high to do that work." [*Journal of Discourses,* Vol. 7, pp. 9-15]   (Continued on page 36.)

---

1. President J. Reuben Clark, Jr., of the First Presidency, *CR*, April, 1957, pp. 44-52.

ORIGINAL SIGNERS OF THE CONSTITUTION OF THE UNITED STATES

Name	Birth Date	Birthplace	State Representing	Age at Convention	Death Date	Occupation
George Washington	Feb. 22, 1732	Popes Creek, Virginia	Virginia	55	Dec. 14, 1799	Farmer
John Langdon	June 26, 1741	Portsmouth, New Hampshire	New Hampshire	46	Sept. 18, 1819	Merchant
Nicholas Gilman	May. 3, 1755	Exeter, New Hampshire	New Hampshire	32	May 2, 1814	Statesman
Nathaniel Gorham	May, 1738	Charleston, Massachusetts	Massachusetts	49	June 11, 1796	Merchant
Rufus King	March 24, 1755	Scarboro, Maine (then part of Mass.)	Massachusetts	32	April 29, 1827	Lawyer
William Samuel Johnson	Oct. 7, 1727	Stratford, Connecticut	Connecticut	59	Nov. 14, 1819	Lawyer
Roger Sherman	April 19, 1721	Newton, Massachusetts	Connecticut	66	July 23, 1793	Merchant
Alexander Hamilton	Jan. 11, 1757	Island of Nevis, West Indies	New York	30	July 12, 1804	Lawyer
William Livingston	Nov. 1723	Albany, New York	New York	63	July 25, 1790	Lawyer
David Brearly	June 11, 1745	Spring Grove, New Jersey	New Jersey	42	Aug. 16, 1790	Lawyer
William Paterson	Dec. 24, 1745	County Antrim, Ireland	New Jersey	41	Sept. 6, 1806	Lawyer
Jonathan Dayton	Oct. 16, 1760	Elizabethtown, New Jersey	New Jersey	26	Oct. 9, 1824	Lawyer
Benjamin Franklin	Jan. 6, 1706	Boston, Massachusetts	Pennsylvania	81	April 17, 1790	Publisher
Thomas Mifflin	Jan. 10, 1744	Philadelphia, Pennsylvania	Pennsylvania	43	Jan. 20, 1800	Merchant
Robert Morris	Jan. 31, 1734	Near Liverpool, England	Pennsylvania	53	May 8, 1806	Financier
George Clymer	March 16, 1739	Philadelphia, Pennsylvania	Pennsylvania	48	Jan. 24, 1813	Merchant
Thomas Fitzsimons	1741	Ireland	Pennsylvania	46	Aug. 26, 1811	Merchant
Jared Ingersoll	Oct. 27, 1749	New Haven, Connecticut	Pennsylvania	38	Oct. 31, 1822	Lawyer
James Wilson	Sept. 14, 1742	Carskerdo, Scotland	Pennsylvania	45	Aug. 21, 1798	Lawyer
George Read	Sept. 18, 1733	North East, Maryland	Delaware	53	Sept. 21, 1798	Lawyer
Gunning Bedford, Jr.	1747	Philadelphia, Pennsylvania	Delaware	40	March 30, 1812	Lawyer
John Dickinson	Nov. 8, 1732	Talbot County, Maryland	Delaware	54	Feb. 14, 1808	Lawyer
Jacob Broom	1752	Wilmington, New Castle Co., Delaware	Delaware	35	April 25, 1810	Statesman
Richard Bassett	April 2, 1745	Cecil County, Maryland	Delaware	42	Sept. 15, 1815	Statesman
James McHenry	Nov. 16, 1753	Ballymena, Ireland	Maryland	33	May 3, 1816	Physician
Daniel of St. Tho. Jenifer	1723	Charles County, Maryland	Maryland	64	Nov. 16, 1790	Financier
Daniel Carroll	July 22, 1730	Upper Marlboro, Maryland	Maryland	57	May 7, 1796	Land Owner
John Blair	1732	Williamsburg, Virginia	Virginia	55	Aug. 31, 1800	Lawyer
James Madison, Jr.	March 16, 1751	Port Conway, Virginia	Virginia	36	June 28, 1836	Lawyer
William Blount	March 26, 1749	Bertie County, North Carolina	North Carolina	38	March 21, 1800	Realtor
Richard Dobbs Spaight	March 25, 1758	New Bern, North Carolina	North Carolina	29	Sept. 6, 1802	Statesman
Hugh Williamson	Oct. 5, 1735	West Nottingham, Pennsylvania	North Carolina	51	May 22, 1819	Physician
John Rutledge	Sept., 1739	Charleston, South Carolina	South Carolina	48	July 18, 1800	Lawyer
Charles Cotesworth Pinckney	Feb. 25, 1746	Charleston, South Carolina	South Carolina	41	Aug. 16, 1825	Lawyer
Charles Pinckney	1758	Charleston, South Carolina	South Carolina	29	Oct. 29, 1824	Lawyer
Pierce Butler	July 11, 1744	County Carlow, Ireland	South Carolina	43	Feb. 15, 1822	Planter
William Few	June 8, 1748	Baltimore, Maryland	Georgia	39	July 16, 1828	Banker
Abraham Baldwin	Nov. 6, 1754	Guilford, Connecticut	Georgia	32	1807	Lawyer

To frail, scholarly *James Madison* of Virginia has been accorded the distinquished title of "Father of the Constitution." Physically and mentally, he was quite different from Washington, being slight of build and never a general but always a brilliant student. Madison, like Washington, however, was favored with a rich religious background which on several occasions shaped his thinking—and that of whole legislative halls.

Madison studied for the ministry. The Hebrew language appealed to him. He "explored the whole history and evidences of Christianity on every side—a feature which bore fruit in his early years in the legislature, freedom of conscience being established by law in Virginia largely by Madison's own labors and influence." [Sarah K. Bolton, *Famous American Statesmen*, pp. 157-158].

He fathered the provisions in Virginia's Bill of Rights, copied by other states: "That religion, or duty we owe to our Creator, and the manner of discharging it, can be directed only by reason and conviction, not by force and violence; and, therefore, all men are equally entitled to the free exercise of religion according to the dictates of conscience."

Elected a member of the first Virginia legislature under its new constitution, Madison "failed of re-election because he refused to solicit votes or to furnish whiskey for thirsty voters." [John Fiske, *Presidents of the United States*, edited by J. G. Wilson, pp. 161-162].

Madison defended free agency in religion in his state on other occasions, and his "Religious Freedom Act," translated into French and Italian, was widely read and commented upon in Europe.

This same Madison, it was, who drew upon the groundwork for the Constitution, who was historiographer for its convention, and who successfully championed its ratification in Virginia in face of such formidable opposition as Patrick Henry and Richard Henry Lee.

No man did more for the Constitution of the United States than did a sandy-haired, handsome little figure with piercing gray-blue eyes, and pointed, classic nose who had come up as a youth to the States from the West Indies. He was *Alexander Hamilton*, who, more than any other, was responsible for the calling of the Constitutional Convention, and who was perhaps its most forceful exponent in bringing about its adoption by the several states.

But thirty of age at the Convention, Hamilton was indeed a prodigy. By the time he was fifteen years old he had worked his way up to the office of assistant manager in a trading business in the Indies. At that age he wrote an account of a hurricane on the islands which won him immediate recognition and the urge of friends to seek fortunes in the colonies.

One of Hamilton's earliest and warmest friends was a Presbyterian minister, the Reverend Hugh Knox, whose teachings no doubt made a lasting impression on the boy. Reverend Knox induced Hamilton to go to the States, and when Alexander departed he took with him a few belongings, including a box of books given him by the minister.

In many respects, Hamilton, as an American, was a modern David. He was fearless, brilliant in expression, full of honor and integrity, though his impetuousness sometimes led him to err. Through his life are incidents which reveal the importance he gave to spiritual affairs.

In 1793, he wrote concerning the French Revolution, which he abhorred: "...When I find the doctrines of atheism openly advanced in the convention with loud applause...when I behold the hand of rapacity outstretched to prostrate and ravish the monuments of religious worship erected by those citizens and their ancestors...I acknowledge that I am glad to believe there is no real semblance between what was the cause of America and what is the cause of France." [Henry Cabot Lodge, *Alexander Hamilton*, pp. 253-254].

Two years before his death, Hamilton, then "an elder statesman" at the age of forty-five, wrote to a friend, James A. Bayard, suggesting methods for building up the Federalist party. In part, he said: "Let an association be formed to be denominated 'The Christian Constitutional Society.' Its objects to be: 1st. The support of the Christian religion. 2nd The support of the Constitution of the United States." [*Ibid.*, p. 264].

When Hamilton's wife, Elizabeth Schuyler Hamilton, died fifty-two years after her husband, a little bag was found tied around her neck. In it was a faded paper containing love verses he had written her seventy-four years before.

Though he was advanced in years, *Benjamin Franklin* gave to the Convention added prestige, profound thought, and its clearest expression of the overruling providence of God at the gathering. Franklin once presented a picturesque explanation of immortality by writing his own epitaph: "The body of Benjamin Franklin, printer, (like the cover of an old book, its contents torn out, and stript of its lettering and gilding), lies here food for worms. Yet the work itself shall not be lost, for it will, as he believed, appear once more, in a new and more beautiful edition, corrected and amended by the Author." [Bernard Fay, *Franklin, The Apostle of Modern Times*, p. 116].

To go down the line of other illustrious personalities signing the Constitution, one finds many examples of characters strengthened by religious experiences. *Roger Sherman*, the only man to sign the four great documents of Revolutionary days (Articles of Association of 1774, Declaration of Independence, Articles of Confederation, and the Constitution), and author of the famous Compromise Plan at the Convention, was a profound student of theology. He published such papers as *A Short Sermon on the Duty of Self-Examination and Pre-paratory to Receiving the Lord's Supper*. A devout Congregationalist, he contributed heavily to the building of the chapel at Yale University. Dr. William Samuel Johnson, another outstanding delegate, studied for the ministry, and his appointment as first president of Columbia College was a departure from the traditional practice of choosing college presidents from the clergy. He was a leading layman in the Anglican Church. David Brearly, representative from New Jersey, was a delegate to the Episcopal General Convention of 1786 and helped compile the prayer book.

Thomas Fitzsimons of Pennsylvania, a strong supporter of Hamilton's views in government, was the largest single contributor to the erection of St. Augustine's Church in Philadelphia, and *Richard Bassett*, who was not only a Constitutional delegate but later served as Delaware's senator (1789-95) and Governor (1799-1801), was an enthusiastic Methodist. He paid approximately half of the cost of the first Methodist Church in Dover.

James McHenry, delegate from Maryland, who had served as major in Washington's army and who was Washington's choice for Secretary of War in 1796, served as president of the first Bible Society founded in Baltimore (1813). *Hugh Williamson,* representative from North Carolina at the Convention, studied theology prior to entering medicine, and was once licensed to preach in Connecticut. He also served in the Continental Congress (1784-6) and in the first United States Congress. A Georgia delegate, *Abraham Baldwin,* was a chaplain in the war. He later was a delegate to the Continental Congress, member of the House of Representatives, and the Senate, and was founder and first president of the University of Georgia.

"He was a staunch believer in revealed religion and a liberal giver of his wealth to all good causes," [*Dictionary of American Biography,* edited by Dumas Malone, Vol. VI, p. 352], is the way one biographer characterizes *William Few,* the other Georgia delegate. He was one of his state's first United States senators.[1]

References to the Latter-day Saint belief in the inspired nature of the Constitution have been made so often and by so many LDS General Authorities that there is no need to compile them in this context. Several examples, however, will serve to indicate the messages which these references usually carry. President George Albert Smith made this statement in the October, 1950 General Conference:

And that brings me to something that is frequently on my mind. *No nation in the world has a constitution that was given to it by our Heavenly Father except the United States of America.* I wonder if we appreciate that. The Lord gave us a rule of life for this great nation, and as far as we have lived up to it and taken advantage of it, the nation has grown, and the people have been blessed.... Why not hold on to what the Lord has given? The Constitution of the United States was written, it is true, by men, George Washington, Benjamin Franklin, and others who were their associates, but we have in this book that I have in my hand, the book of Doctrine and Covenants, *a revelation in which the Lord tells us that the Constitution of the Church was prepared by men raised up by him for this very purpose.*

As Latter-day Saints we ought to know that there is nothing better anywhere else. And so *we should cleave to the Constitution of the United States and in doing so, earn the blessings of our Heavenly Father....* The Constitution guarantees us liberty that no other nation enjoys. Most of the nations are losing the liberties they have because they have not kept the commandments of the Lord.... I hold in my hand a copy of the Doctrine and Covenants, and in it the Lord tells us another thing, to pray for and sustain the Constitution of the land and those who represent us in its offices. So, *pray for the President of the United States, pray for those who have been elected to Congress, pray*

---

1. Wendell J. Ashton, General Secretary, Deseret Sunday School Union, "The Signers of the Constitution," *IE,* Vol. 45, No. 9, September, 1942, pp. 562-563, 598-600.

for your governor and the members of your legislature. If they have the spirit of the Lord, they cannot go wrong; but without it they can go a long way on the bypath.[1]

While telling of one man's love and allegiance to the United States, Elder Thorpe B. Isaacson again asserted the LDS doctrine that the Constitution is an inspired document:

I ask each of you now to consider with me for a few moments one of our most precious possessions—our citizenship in the United States of America, this nation under God.

A very fine man who came to the United States a few years ago from a foreign country and who now has his citizenship papers remarked to me that next to God and his loved ones, he considered his citizenship in the United States as his most precious and priceless possession. Yes, his most precious and priceless possession. *He said he loved the United States and was grateful for the freedom that it afforded him, because, you see, he had lived in a country where he did not know that freedom. When he said that he loved the United States and that he thanked God for his citizenship in this country, he said it with every fiber of his soul. He said he would fight for this country and this freedom, even if it meant his own life. He said that every citizen of the United States ought to feel that way; and if he did feel that way, talked that way, and loved that way, we would have no problem from within and no fear from without.* Yes, this nation under God means exactly what it says.

Let me quote from the Doctrine and Covenants:

"Let no man break the laws of the land, for he that keepeth the laws of God hath no need to break the laws of the land." [D & C 58:2.]

The Constitution of the United States is a document from inspired men. On August 6, 1833, the Church received a revelation that has gone far to establish a fixed attitude toward the Constitution and laws of the United States. Then came the word of the Lord:

"And now, verily I say unto you concerning the laws of the land, it is my will that my people should observe to do all things whatsoever I command them." [*Ibid.,* 101:79.]

Man could not so act save he live in a land of law, for only in a land of law can there be freedom as we know it.

"And for this purpose have I established the Constitution of this land, by the hands of wise men whom I raised up unto this very purpose, and redeemed the land by the shedding of blood." [*Ibid.,* 101:80.]

This revelation has a powerful influence in shaping the views of Latter-day Saints toward the Constitution of the United States, and it should also have a great influence on every citizen, for the *Lord suffered it to be by the hands of wise men.*[2]

---

1. President George Albert Smith, President of the Church, *CR*, September, 1950, pp. 7-8.
2. Elder Thorpe B. Isaacson, Assistant to the Council of the Twelve, *CR*, October, 1964, pp. 52-53.

Summary

1.   Latter-day Saints hold as doctrine the belief that the American continents constitute a land which God has declared to be choice and consecrated above all other lands. This belief is often applied to the United States of America in particular.

2.   The Americas were pledged by God as a land of inheritance to Lehi's descendants forever (2 Ne. 1:5-7). They are descendants of Joseph who was sold into Egypt (the son of the Old Testament patriarch, Jacob). The Americas will constitute a place of inheritance for a portion of the house of Joseph in the last days (Eth. 13:6-8). Because of this pledge, the Americas are considered a land of promise.

3.   Because of a vision given to the prophet Nephi (1 Ne. 12 & 13) Latter-day Saint teachings include the beliefs that

> A.   Columbus was inspired by God to sail to America,
> B.   Early American settlers were inspired by God to leave their European homes and come to America,
> C.   Early American settlers were caused by God to prosper here. His power was with them,
> D.   God delivered America so it became independent, and that
> E.   God lifted America above all other nations.

4.   Latter-day Saint General Authorities frequently speak on themes of liberty and patriotism. Love and concern for country is a characteristic of the leadership of The Church of Jesus Christ of Latter-day Saints.

5.   A frequent approach used by LDS General Authorities is to quote statements from non-LDS historical or modern sources which indicate that there was divine guidance in the founding of the United States of America.

6.   Numerous founding fathers of America have given indication that they were aware of God's guiding hand in the formulative events of this nation's early history. Some of their statements are included in this book.

7.   The Lord has revealed that He established the U.S. Constitution and raised up wise men for the very purpose of bringing

it forth. He has instructed the Saints to befriend the Constitutional law of the land.

8.   A discourse by J. Reuben Clark, Jr. emphasized important aspects of the Constitution. These include

A.   The Constitution provides for three independent departments of government—the legislative, the executive, and the judicial.

B.   Each of the three departments of government are to remain separate and are not to encroach upon the duties of another branch. This separation is to provide a system of "checks and balances."

C.   None of the three departments can delegate its powers to the others.

D.   As chief executive, the President is to execute the laws passed by Congress.

E.   The President was not given the power to declare war. That power was given to Congress.

F.   The President is the commander-in-chief of the army and the navy and is to direct their activities in time of war.

G.   The people of the nation are sovereign. They possess all the powers except those they have delegated to the government.

II

What's Right With America?

What's right with America? What freedoms do we enjoy? Americans would do well to consider these questions, and compare what they have to the conditions they would experience living in other parts of the world.

Imagine—what would your life be like if you lived under the political repression of the Soviet Union, or Red China, or East Germany? How would you fare if you lived under the jurisdiction of military dictators in South America, with their unbelievably sky-rocketing inflation? Or what would life be like in the poverty-stricken hands of rural Central America? Would you rather be in the midst of Africa's young nations, with tribal and racial wars an imminent prospect? What if the size of your family was limited by law, as in some of the Asian countries? Think back in time just one generation—would you have enjoyed the midnight abductions and reign of terror of Germany's Gestapo? or the Jewish pogroms? the Warsaw ghetto? Austwitz? life in occupied France, or Holland? Imagine! Compare!

The United States of America is truly a land of freedom. It is a nation with a great heritage, an inspiring history, and the potential for a glorious future. Settled by a unique mixture of freedom-loving peoples, it has been the symbol of hope and opportunity for the inhabitants of planet earth for more than two hundred years.

Its Constitution and government have served as models for emerging nations. The free enterprise economic system it fostered has made a vast panorama of goods and services available throughout the world, providing its citizens with a standard of living unparalleled until the past decade. Education has been fostered and creativity encouraged, resulting in an overwhelming array of unique inventions and technological advances. The land itself is a place of beauty—a fruitful land bringing forth rich harvests and yielding tremendous quantities of mineral wealth.

The nation's sovereignty has been protected, its continental borders have been shielded from invasion, its armies have been victorious in war. Truly America has been a God-protected land "blessed with victory and peace."[1]

---

1. Francis Scott Key, "The Star Spangled Banner," verse 4.

Though the liberties and privileges enjoyed in America are so abundant as to almost defy enumeration, it is appropriate that some basic freedoms and opportunities be recalled as a reminder to all that they form the basis for the happy and abundant life Americans enjoy. Indeed, these freedoms are what make life worth living.

Freedom of Worship

America has no state religion to which its citizens must belong, and the establishment of a prescribed religion is expressly prohibited by the Constitution.[1] The preaching of any and all religious philosophies, and the free exercise of religion, is a liberty guaranteed by law. Churches may proselyte freely and assemble when and where they desire without the necessity of government permission. They may build chapels, seminaries, and temples, subject only to the necessary regulation of local building codes, and the sanctity of these edifices is held inviolate by government officials. Church schools and universities may be established and operated on either a denominational or an open basis.

Religious and denominational literature can be freely written and disseminated without censorship, and is readily available in bookstores open to the public. The Bible is available in many editions and is even used as a measure of integrity in oaths taken in courts of law and in the swearing in of public officials. Religious sermons and related programming are heard on local and national radio and television. Churches can advertise in newspapers and other media.

The growth and well-being of religious institutions are encouraged by property and income tax exemptions which foster charitable donations. The uplifting influence of religion is accepted as an important element of community life, and religious officers hold positions of respect in communities throughout the nation.

Thus Americans have the privilege of worshipping according to the dictates of their own conscience, in full application of their God-given moral agency.

Freedom of Speech

Liberty to hold and publicly express one's personal views is a vital freedom enjoyed by American citizens. To be able to speak in support of one's beliefs on any subject without fear of governmental, social, or economic reprisal is a privilege not enjoyed in

---

1. Constitution of the United States, Amendments, Article I.

many other parts of the world. Americans enjoy the right to dissent from governmental policies if they so desire, and are free to work by a variety of lawful means to bring about change from laws and decisions which they may feel are improper or unjust. They are free to visit with or write to governmental leaders, to write and publish even materials which are critical of government policies, and to openly organize and influence others to accomplish their own ends. The privilege of free speech is a liberty which is soon lost under dictatorial and despotic governments. In a democracy, it serves as a check and balance to prevent governmental excesses or corruption.

Freedom of the Press and News Media

A free press and news media serve as powerful watchdogs, monitoring and reporting events of importance and concern to the community at large. Americans enjoy the right of having newspapers, television, radio, and other media owned and controlled by private rather than government sources. Thus the journalistic media are not instruments of official propaganda, but are independent institutions[1] that can examine issues from various viewpoints, expose improprieties, command accomplishments, and report bureaucratic weaknesses and failures when necessary. Their independent voices allow the citizenry to see and evaluate issues with perspective.

Columnists and editors present a host of viewpoints on major issues, exposing their readers to a broad spectrum of thought. Readers also enjoy the same intellectual freedom, being encouraged to respond with letters to the editor which are frequently published.

The media sometimes serve as catalysts, organizing community efforts to accomplish important objectives, or stimulating the masses to correct inequities at the polls.

A free press and news media serve as an effective check on governmental improprieties. They are essential to the maintenance of the nation's most fundamental liberties.

Freedom of Assembly

The right of the people peaceably to assemble is another liberty guaranteed in the Constitution.[2] Americans are free to

---

1. Constitution of the United States, Amendments, Article I.
2. *Ibid.*

meet together in groups for any purpose—religious, political, social, recreational, educational, or any other—without prior governmental consent. Such a privilege is quickly lost under a dictorial regime, where the right to assemble is almost always suppressed.

Freedom to Petition for Governmental Redress

The right to petition the government for a redress of grievances is another liberty expressly stipulated in the Constitution.[1] In many instances a private citizen or company may sue a local, state, or national government body for redress. Assistance can also be sought through communication with elected representatives who will work to sponsor and pass corrective legislation. In principle, government agencies and officials are responsible for their actions under the law just as are private citizens.

Freedom to Bear Arms

The U.S. Constitution also stipulates that "the right of the people to keep and bear Arms, shall not be infringed."[2] American citizens have the right to own guns both for sport and for purposes of personal protection.

Freedom from Unlawful Quartering of Soldiers in Private Homes

No soldier can be quartered in a private home during peacetime without the consent of the owner of the home, according to the Constitution.[3] The same prohibition exists in times of war, though soldiers can be stationed in private homes in wartime if it is done in a manner prescribed by law.

Freedom from Unreasonable Searches and Seizures

Citizens have the right to be secure from unauthorized searches and seizures in their persons, houses, papers, and effects.[4] Law enforcement officials must first obtain a warrant which particularly describes the place to be searched and the person or things to be seized. Such warrants are to be issued only when there is probable cause and when supported by an oath or affirmation.

---

1. *Ibid.*
2. *Ibid.*, Article II.
3. *Ibid.*, Article III.
4. *Ibid.*, Article IV.

Freedom from Imprisonment without Indictment

Citizens are protected from extended imprisonment unless a formal indictment is made charging them with a specific capital or infamous crime.[1] (Exceptions exist to this liberty in the military forces or militia during time of war or public danger.)

Freedom from Double Jeopardy

The Constitution guarantees that no person shall "be subject for the same offense to be twice put in jeopardy of life of limb."[2] If tried and acquitted for a crime, he cannot again be tried for the same offense.

Freedom from Forced Confession

Every citizen has the right to be silent and to refrain from any act or statement of self-incrimination in a criminal case. The Constitution expressly prohibits any situation in which an individual might be compelled to be a witness against himself.[3]

Freedom from Punishment without Due Process of Law

Another constitutional guarantee is that an individual shall "not be deprived of life, liberty, or property, without due process of law."[4] Thus a person cannot be fined, imprisoned, or executed unless found guilty in an authorized court of law.

Freedom from Public Confiscation without Renumeration

Yet another freedom enjoyed in America is the guarantee that an individual's private property shall not be taken for public use without just compensation being paid to him.[5] While a government body is considered to have sovereign power over all lands within its jurisdiction through the right of eminent domain, property owners are entitled to just payment for the property taken in such instances.

Freedom from Improper Trials

The U.S. Constitution guarantees a series of rights in connection with trial procedures in criminal prosecutions. An accused

---

1. *Ibid.*, Article V.
2. *Ibid.*
3. *Ibid.*
4. *Ibid.*
5. *Ibid.*

party is entitled to a "speedy and public trial,"[1] and to be judged by an impartial jury from the state and district where the alleged crime was committed. The accused person is entitled to be informed of the nature and cause of the accusation. The accused is to be confronted with the witnesses against him.[2]

If a person is accused and brought to trial, he is entitled to have compulsory process for obtaining witnesses in his favor. He also has the right to have legal counsel to assist him in his defense.[3]

In common law suits where the value in controversy exceeds twenty dollars, an accused person is entitled to a jury trial, and no fact tried by a jury can be otherwise re-examined in any court of the United States except according to the rules of common law.[4]

Freedom from Excessive Bail

The U.S. Constitution stipulates that "excessive bail shall not be required."[5] Thus bail must be fixed in a manner proportional to the seriousness of the crime for which an individual has been charged.

Freedom from Excessive Fines

A further Constitutional guarantee is that excessive fines shall not be imposed as payment for crimes for which individuals have been found guilty.[6] A balance is to be maintained between the seriousness of the crime and the degree of punishment meted out to the offender.

Freedom from Cruel and Unusual Punishments

An important liberty enjoyed by Americans is the guarantee that cruel or unusual punishments will not be inflicted upon them.[7] Torture, beatings, and similar mistreatments are prohibited and, if they do occur, are punishable by law.

Freedom from Slavery or Involuntary Servitude

Slavery or involuntary servitude, except as a punishment for a crime whereof the party shall have been duly convicted, is

---

1. *Ibid.*, Article VI.
2. *Ibid.*
3. *Ibid.*
4. *Ibid.*, Article VII.

5. *Ibid.*, Article VIII.
6. *Ibid.*
7. *Ibid.*

prohibited in the United States or any place within U.S. juris-diction.[1]

Freedom from State Laws Abridging Citizenship Rights

The Constitution prohibits the making or enforcing of any state law which would abridge the privileges or immunities granted under the Constitution to citizens of the United States.[2] No state is allowed to deprive any person of life, liberty or property without due process of law, nor deny to any person within its jurisdiction the equal protection of the laws.

Freedom to Vote

The Constitution stipulates that neither the United States nor any state can deny or abridge the right of any citizen to vote because of his race, color, sex, or previous condition of servitude.[3]

American citizens enjoy the right to vote by secret ballot for local, state, and national officials and to choose through the ballot many of the laws which will be established.

The election system provides for a constant re-selection of leaders and serves to prevent the establishment of dictatorial pow-ers. All citizens registered to vote are entitled to a part in choosing government officials. They are free to vote ineffective or incompe-tent men out of office and to pursue necessary reforms by peaceful and proper methods. This system of changeable leadership reduces the possibility of government corruption and of unjust govern-mental intervention into the private affairs of the citizenry.

Freedom to Hold Public Office

American citizens are eligible to run for and be elected to public office, subject only to minimum eligibility requirements such as citizenship, residence, age, etc. They may also form new political parties, campaign actively for themselves or others, and establish any political ideological platform which they deem to be appropriate.

Freedom to Own and Accumulate Property

The right to own and acquire property and tangible assets is a fundamental liberty enjoyed by Americans. Indeed, it stands as the

---

1. *Ibid.*, Article XIII.
2. *Ibid.*, Article XIV, Section I.
3. *Ibid.*, Article XV, Section I.

key to the nation's vast economic system based on free enterprise. The privilege of ownership has been the stimulus and driving motivation for many who have immigrated to America's shores. It was the hope that moved homesteaders to settle virgin tracts and inspired pioneers to forge new lives in the west.

Freedom of Information

The right of Americans to have access to public records is another important liberty which adds stability to the nation and serves as a balancing influence. Government bodies are accountable for their actions, their policies, and their use of public monies. Citizen access to their records allows inspection and evaluation which will detect evidence of wrongdoing if such exists.

Historical records are also available, allowing a true transmittal of the American heritage without the intrusion of propaganda.

Americans are entitled to access to their own credit files, government dossiers, criminal records and other documents which comment upon their personal lives and habits. This gives them opportunity to correct misinformation which may have been erroneously added to the files.

Information of a general and educational nature is also readily available through libraries, bookstores, and the corner marketplace. Americans can read what they want, without having to participate in mandatory indoctrination programs established by government agencies.

Freedom of Communication

Americans enjoy the liberty to communicate with anyone they please throughout the world. Modern technology has extended the scope of this privilege, providing sophisticated telephone, telegraph, radio, satellite, and other equipment to speed the communication process.

Letters and packages can be sent through the mails with the expectation that the missives will arrive without being censored, tampered with, or stolen, a privilege not enjoyed in many countries today.

Freedom of Privacy

As modern living becomes more complex, increased protection is being given to insure individual privacy. Legislation has been enacted to guarantee American citizens protection against improper phone tapping, "bugging" and other electronic surveillance, and government scrutiny of foreign mail that might be politically sensitive. Controls have been set to protect citizens from unwarranted spying by the FBI and the CIA. Citizens have been given the right to inspect files kept about them by government agencies, local law enforcement officials, credit reporting firms, and others who may be maintaining records concerning their activities.

Freedom to Travel

Americans enjoy freedom to travel throughout the country without having to obtain governmental permission or having to pass through regulatory checkpoints. They can go where they want and do so when they please, without being bothered or influenced by stifling government regulations. Freedom to travel in America is enhanced by the high quality of the vast transportation network which stretches across the nation. Good highways, the easy availability of gasoline and service stations, and quality automobiles priced within the economic reach of the average citizen, increase the nation's mobility. Transportation networks have made air, bus, rail, and ship travel available to the masses. Municipal transit networks have also made local travel a reality in the nation's cities.

Travel abroad is easily undertaken also, with passports and visas readily obtainable.

Freedom to Choose Place of Residence

In this great land, people are free to choose their place of residence without the prohibiting influence of government controls. Caste, race, creed, or color do not provide bases for determining housing locations, nor do they affect zoning ordinances designed to protect the lifestyle and economic value of local subdivisions and neighborhoods. Citizens are free to move from state to state to obtain new employment or to meet other personal needs.

Americans can even move to foreign countries, taking up either temporary or permanent residence there, without jeopardizing the safety and well-being of family members who remain behind. These privileges are also extended to students and visitors from other countries who come to the United States.

Freedom of Education

Americans enjoy the right to gain a basic education in free public schools. This schooling, on both the primary and secondary levels, is available to all. Parents and youth have a voice in determining educational policies and curriculum, and local schoolboards are subject to community guidance, both through individual input and through the elective process. Schools can determine their curricula and texts without government censorship.

No government tests limit the amount or kind of schooling one may obtain, nor are students compelled to pursue careers deemed important by the state. Students are able to pursue advanced studies at a broad variety of universities and trade schools across the nation. Many scholarships, grants, and loans are available to assist needy and worthy students. College-level scholars are free to choose their major fields. They can change their courses, if they desire, and they can pursue their studies as long as they wish, subject only to their personal, scholastic, time, and economic limitations.

Freedom to Choose Medical Care

Under the American free enterprize system, citizens can exercise their personal choice in selecting doctors and dentists to administer to their physical needs—no government bureaucracy makes this choice for them. Both general practitioners and specialists are available within a reasonable travel distance of almost every community, as are hospitals and other advanced medical facilities. A wide spectrum of medicines and drugs is available. The American people are free from many of the diseases which wreck havoc in other parts of the world because of their progress in sanitation facilities, food processing technology, availability of adequate food supply, environmental care, etc.

Freedom from Want

Food, clothing, and other basic necessities are in plentiful supply in America. Citizens are able to obtain the goods needed to sustain life without having to wait in long lines or having them rationed. Fewer hours of work are required to earn the price of goods in the United States than in most other countries,[1] and

(Continued on p. 53.)

---

1. Dr. Joseph S. Peery, a professor of economics in the College of Business at the University of Utah, while speaking on the patriotic series presented in Utah's KSL radio and TV series, "What's Right With America?,"

added statistical insights to demonstrate the abundance enjoyed in this nation. He commented:

"American farms are unbelievably productive. Only 4% of our work force is in agriculture. In France it is 18%, in Japan 24%, in Russia 33%. We Americans spend a smaller part of our income on food than do any other people. We have the most varied diets, and the greatest surplus of food." (Program aired August 12, 1976.)

"A typical factory worker in the United States has to pay an equivalent of 4 years wages to buy a small house. In England the same worker would have to work 6 years, in France 8 years, and in West Germany 10 years. We Americans are the best housed in the world and it is only because our free market system is, by far, the most productive on earth." (Program aired July 24, 1976.)

"Food is a bargain for Americans. We spend only 17% of our income on food. In England and France, food consumes a quarter of total income; in Germany 32%; in Eastern Europe and Russia 40%. Food costs us less and we have the richest and most varied diet on earth." (Program aired May 24, 1976.)

"The 1976 standard of living of the average American family is twice as high as it was at the end of World War II; four times as high as it was in 1900; and over ten times as high as it was in 1776. The American system has produced affluence undreamed of by the founders of this country." (Program aired July 31, 1976.)

"The opportunity for college training really exists in this country. Over 20% of the young people who come from poverty homes with incomes below $5,000 a year are now enrolled in college. This is a higher percentage than the total rate for France, Germany, England, and Italy. Here, the children of all income groups have a greater chance to go to college than in any other country." (Program aired July 21, 1976.)

"Real family income has doubled in this country in the past 28 years, and that's with inflation removed. More than one-half of all American families now have incomes over $13,000 a year. We have a standard of living that is the envy of the whole world." (Program aired May 10, 1976.)

"Nine out of every 10 American families have radios, TV sets, automatic coffee makers, vacuum cleaners, and hot and cold running water. More than half of our homes are air conditioned and 40% of us have more than one car. All this in a world, where for most people, pure water alone is a luxury. Let's appreciate the good life we Americans have. It is the best in the world." (Program aired June 16, 1976.)

Others have added further insights. Booth Wallentine, executive vice president of the Utah Farm Bureau, observed that "America's two million farms and ranches produce enough food for nearly 23% of the world." (Program aired May 5, 1976.) Bob Halladay, executive vice president of the Utah Manufacturers Association, told of the nation's move towards affluence: "In 1959, one-fifth of all Americans were living below the poverty line. Now the total is half that and is still falling. The United States has the largest middle income class in the world." (Program aired July 16, 1976.)

many Americans have ample leisure time in addition to the time required to earn a living. Farming, food processing, transportation, and other related industries are so advanced that specialty foods grown only in limited areas are available to consumers throughout the nation.

Housing is available. Americans can build or buy a home, or remodel existing edifices if they choose to do so.

Automobiles, home appliances, and a wide variety of consumer goods are found in well-stocked stores across the land for all who wish to purchase them.

Electricity, natural gas, and telephone systems extend to homes across the country, making the use of home appliances practical.

The availability of consumer goods, plus economic conditions which allow ordinary citizens the discretionary income to purchase them in abundance, have combined to give Americans a high standard of living and an almost universal freedom from want of the basic commodities needed to sustain life.

Freedom of Vocational Choice

Unlike many other countries where vocational choices are limited because of government policy or severe economic conditions, America is still a "land of opportunity" where individuals may choose and pursue the vocational objectives which will best meet their personal needs. The free enterprize system is far-reaching in the vocational potential it offers. Individuals may choose whether to be self-employed or to work for others, and may select vocational goals from a broad spectrum. University, trade school, and on-the-job training programs make it possible for workers to learn the necessary skills. Laws prevent the exploitation of child laborers and require that acceptable working conditions be maintained. Freedom to move from one area to another also gives workers increased control over their vocational growth.

Freedom Through Economic Stability

Closely linked with the benefits of free vocational choice are privileges derived from America's economic system. Americans are able to invest their earnings, having confidence in the stability of their currency and banking system. They can save to meet future needs, investing with a reasonable hope and expectation of eventual profit. A consumer credit system makes the purchase of goods on a time-payment or credit card basis possible, thereby opening access to many purchases which would otherwise be impossible for many consumers to make. Capital is available for business investments, which eventually results in more goods being available in the well-stocked stores which are the envy of other nations around the world. The stability of the American economy makes it possible for the free enterprize system to flourish and for the people to enjoy the fruits of prosperity.

Freedom Through Social Acceptance

America takes pride in its role as the "melting pot" which has accepted immigrants from throughout the world. No rigid caste or social stratification system exists in this country. Opportunity for employment, schooling, housing, and personal growth exists for those of all ethnic and religious backgrounds. Though some integration problems may still exist, great strides have been made towards the elimination of discriminating practices based on race, religion, sex, or age. People can live in the neighborhood of their choice. A wide range of dress styles and standards is accepted. Varied art, folk, and traditional practices are maintained as people preserve the memories of their former cultures. Young people are free to marry whom they wish, even crossing over racial bounds. Individuals can choose their friends and associates, and are free to talk and openly discuss any matter they choose. Americans can trust and confide in one another, without fear that their neighbors are spies who will report their comments to critical police authorities. Social acceptance and equality of opportunity in America are choice liberties which add much to the value of life.

Freedom of Family Life

Americans are free to choose the family lifestyle they wish to pursue. Parents may determine the size of their families without having to submit to government population controls. Mothers can remain in the home and raise their own children, without being compelled to leave and work at government-assigned tasks. Children are not required to be raised in government-established nurseries. The family unit is still the basic building block of American society. Parents are free to teach their children moral and religious values and precepts. Schools are not government propaganda agents committed to a mission of political indoctrination. In the typical American home there are moments of leisure time and family recreation opportunities—the state makes no demand on one's time.

Freedom Through Police Protection

In America the police are regarded as the citizens' protectors and helpers rather than their enemies. Most communities have an efficient, high-quality police force comprised of competent officers who feel real concern for the well-being of residents in their jurisdictional area. Citizens expect their property and persons to be protected under the provisions of the law. In general, they are able to feel peace of mind and an attitude of security and safety. They see in the due process of law a system through which they can properly demand justice and receive redress for grievances they may receive. An effective police force, dedicated to the preservation of law and order, provides citizens with liberty and safety not found where government corruption or anarchy prevail.

Freedom of Artistic Expression

In America artists are free to draw what they choose. Performers can play music from any composer, or any style, without government restraint. Authors can write on the subjects of their choice. There are no forbidden subjects, or styles, or composers which they must avoid.

Freedom of Scientific Discovery

Research can be conducted in any field in private laboratories and in university facilities. No government prohibitions inhibit the continuing quest for knowledge or require inventors and scientists to avoid particular areas of exploration and investigation. Researchers can contribute to the best of their ability without government restraint.

Freedom to Limit Government

The framers of the Constitution recognized that government was to be the servant, not the master of the people. Though they used that inspired document to establish many of man's basic freedoms, they expressly stipulated that "the enumeration in the Constitution, of certain rights, shall not be construed to deny or disparage others retained by the people."[1] They also provided that

---

1. Constitution, *op. cit.*, Amendments, Article IX.

"The powers not delegated to the United States by the Constitution, nor prohibited by it to the States, are reserved to the States respectively, or to the people."[1]

The people, then, maintain the rights not specifically relegated to government. Theirs is the individual right through judicial suit, or collective right through the ballot box, to limit government if it begins to encroach upon their liberties. In the Constitutional plan, they are the masters. Power over government is theirs, if they will but use it.

Summary

America is a great nation, with stability and direction. Laws set forth at the highest level provide checks and balances which protect every man from a host of possible abuses. The pattern set forth in the Constitution has enabled the common man to maintain dignity, to work to achieve personal goals, and to resist the encroachment of tyranny.

1. To perceive the extent of the great freedoms enjoyed by American citizens, one has but to compare life in the United States with conditions in other countries throughout the world.

2. Many freedoms enjoyed by U.S. citizens were listed, including:

    A.   Freedom of worship.
    B.   Freedom of speech.
    C.   Freedom of press and news media.
    D.   Freedom of assembly.
    E.   Freedom of petition for governmental redress.
    F.   Freedom to bear arms.
    G.   Freedom from unlawful quartering of soldiers in private homes.
    H.   Freedom from unreasonable searches and seizures.
    I.   Freedom from imprisonment without indictment.
    J.   Freedom from double jeopardy.
    K.   Freedom from forced confession.
    L.   Freedom from punishment without due process of law.
    M.   Freedom from public confiscation without renumeration.

---

1. *Ibid.*, Article X.

N.   Freedom from improper trials.

O.   Freedom from excessive bail.

P.   Freedom from excessive fines.

Q.   Freedom from cruel and unusual punishments.

R.   Freedom from slavery or involuntary servitude.

S.   Freedom from state laws abridging citizenship rights.

T.   Freedom to vote.

U.   Freedom to hold public office.

V.   Freedom to own and accumulate property.

W.   Freedom of information.

X.   Freedom of communication.

Y.   Freedom of privacy.

Z.   Freedom to travel.

AA.   Freedom to choose place of residence.

BB.   Freedom of education.

CC.   Freedom to choose medical care.

DD.   Freedom from want.

EE.   Freedom of vocational choice.

FF.   Freedom through economic stability.

GG.   Freedom through social acceptance.

HH.   Freedom of family life.

II.   Freedom through police protection.

JJ.   Freedom of artistic expression.

KK.   Freedom of scientific discovery.

LL.   Freedom to limit government.

Choosing a Course for the Future

III

Personal Preparation for the Last Days

America stands at the crossroads! The last three decades have been a period of serious moral decay for the nation, and wickedness has spread rapidly. Crime, violence, and immorality have become commonplace. There truly is significant cause for concern over the future of this great nation.

The warning fo the Book of Mormon prophet Alma, typical of many scriptural warnings about the future of America,[1] gives reason for significant concern:

> ...Thus saith the Lord God—*cursed shall be the land, yea, this land, unto every nation, kindred, tongue, and people, unto destruction, which do wickedly, when they are fully ripe*; and as I have said so shall it be; for this is the cursing and the blessing upon the land, for the Lord cannot look upon sin with the least degree of allowance.[2]

Joseph Smith's famous prophecy on war fortells a series of wars which began with the U.S. Civil War, which will continue "until the consumption decreed hath made a full end of all nations."[3] With scriptural revelation warning that this land will undergo future wars and cataclysmic events, thoughtful Church members want to know they can help America escape the most severe effects of the prophesied judgments, and how they can personally prepare. This chapter suggests essential actions American Latter-day Saints should undertake to prepare for the challenging events of the future. It should be oberved that every principle suggested is based on counsel and insight God has revealed in the scriptures.

Adopt Attitudes Based on Gospel Principles

The gospel of Jesus Christ provides instruction and insight, telling man how he should conduct himself during the perilous era of the last days. If he will adopt the eternal perspectives revealed in the gospel plan, he will "build his house upon a rock," rather than upon sand,[4] and have stability and meaning to life as the

---

1. See *Inspired Prophetic Warnings*, pp. 27-158.
2. Al. 45:16. See also D & C 1:31; Al. 37:28, 31.
3. D & C 87:6.
4. See Mt. 7:24-27.

judgments are poured out. This section will suggest attitudes and understandings which should prove beneficial.

1. Gain eternal perspective: God directs the affairs of man. There is comfort in the knowledge that God, who created the earth and made man after his own image,[1] sees and knows all things.[2] "All things are before him,"[3] and he "governeth and executeth all things."[4] Though he allows man to exercise his free agency,[5] he maintains ultimate control over the actions and fate of both individuals and nations.[6] He has promised to guide and shape the course of those who live righteously, and has instructed the saints to "let your hearts be comforted; *for all things shall work together for good to them that walk uprightly.*"[7]

2. Gain eternal perspective: God desires to bless and reward man. God seeks the eternal progress and well-being of his people. He has revealed that "this is my work and my glory—to bring to pass the immortality and eternal life of man."[8] The Savior has told the saints they are *"ye whom I delight to bless with the greatest of all blessings, ye that hear me;"*[9] and he has said:

> I, the Lord, am merciful and gracious unto those who fear me, and *delight to honor those who serve me* in righteousness and in truth unto the end.
> *Great shall be their reward and eternal shall be their glory.*[10]

He has said to his people that the fulness of the earth is theirs to use and enjoy, and that "it pleaseth God that he hath given all these things unto man."[11] He would extend his richest blessings to all mankind if they would only accept his overtures:

---

1. D & C 20:17-18.
2. D & C 38:1-3.
3. D & C 88:41.
4. D & C 88:40.
5. D & C 58:28; 104:17.
6. For extensive listings of examples concerning this principle, see the author's book *Prophets and Prophecies of the Old Testament*, p. 91.
7. D & C 100:15. As Paul taught, "All things work together for good to them that love God." (Ro. 8:28) See also D & C 90:24; 105:40; 111:11.
8. Moses 1:39.
9. D & C 41:1. But the same verse contains a strong warning to the saints: saying that *"Ye that hear me not will I curse,* that have professed my name, with the heaviest of all cursings."
10. D & C 76:5-6. Verses 7-10 promise choice blessings to these individuals.
11. D & C 59:16-21.

O, ye nations of the earth, how often would I have gathered you together as a hen gathereth her chickens under her wings, but ye would not!

How oft have I called upon you...by the voice of mercy all the day long, and by the voice of glory and honor and the riches of eternal life, and *would have saved you with an everlasting salvation, but ye would not!*[1]

3. Gain eternal perspective: Last days' judgments are part of man's mortal probation. The prophet Alma explained the probationary nature of mortal life, saying that

...There was a space granted unto man in which he might repent; therefore *this life became a probationary state; a time to prepare to meet God;* a time to prepare for that endless state which has been spoken of by us, which is after the resurrection of the dead.[2]

God has revealed to the saints that they must be tested and refined through that testing process:

...I have decreed in my heart, saith the Lord, that *I will prove you in all things, whether you will abide in my covenant, even unto death, that you may be found worthy.*

For if ye will not abide in my covenant ye are not worthy of me.[3]

Indeed, remaining faithful in tribulation appears to be a necessary requirement for gaining the highest of eternal rewards. A revelation from the Lord teaches that

...Blessed is he that keepeth my commandments, whether in life or in death; and *he that is faithful in tribulation, the reward of the same is greater in the kingdom of heaven.*

Ye cannot behold with your natural eyes, for the present time, the design of your God concerning those things which shall come hereafter, and *the glory which shall follow after much tribulation.*

For after much tribulation come the blessings. Wherefore the day cometh that ye shall be crowned with much glory; the hour is not yet, but is nigh at hand.[4]

4. Gain eternal perspective: God chastens those he loves. Our Heavenly Father loves his children who are here on earth. His son,

1. D & C 43:24-25. See Mt. 23:37.
2. Al. 12:24. See also 2 Ne. 2:21; 9:27; 33:9; Al. 42:4; Hel. 13:38; D & C 29:42-44.
3. D & C 98:14-15.
4. D & C 58:2-4. See also D & C 103:11-14.

Jesus Christ, also loves his people—those who are "children of Christ" through the gospel covenant.[1] Like any loving parent, they seek to teach and encourage man, sometimes correcting his conduct and directing him towards the proper course of behavior.

This correcting process will be a part of the judgments of the last days and will ultimately prove to be a blessing for the saints who heed the warning message. The Master has revealed,

> Verily, thus saith the Lord unto you whom I love, and *whom I love I also chasten that their sins may be forgiven,* for with the chastisement *I prepare a way for their deliverance* in all things out of temptation....[2]

He has said that

> *My people must be tried in all things,* that they may be prepared to receive the glory that I have for them, even the glory of Zion; and *he that will not bear chastisement is not worthy of my kingdom.*[3]

The chastening process has previously been experienced in the Church in connection with the failure to properly establish the New Jerusalem. Yet "Zion shall be redeemed, although she is chastened for a little season."[4] The early problem concerning Jackson County, in which the saints were driven out by their enemies, provided the basis for a revelation in which the Lord explained the relationship between chastening and the sanctification process:

> Verily I say unto you, concerning your brethren who have been afflicted, and persecuted, and cast out from the land of their inheritance—
> *I, the Lord, have suffered the affliction to come upon them, wherewith they have been afflicted, in consequence of their transgressions;*
> Yet I will own them, and they shall be mine in that day when I shall come to make up my jewels.
> Therefore, they must needs be chastened and tried, even as Abraham, who was commanded to offer up his only son.
> *For all those who will not endure chastening, but deny me, cannot be sanctified.*[5]

The saints must obtain confidence that the chastening which will come will ultimately bless them if they endure it in faith. As the Lord told Joseph Smith concerning the great tribulations he suffered:

---

1. See Mos. 5:5-7.
2. D & C 95:1.
3. D & C 136:31.

4. D & C 100:13. See D & C 103:4.
5. D & C 101:1-5.

...Know thou, my son, that *all these things shall give thee experience,
and shall be for thy good.*

The Son of Man hath descended below them all. Art thou greater
than he?[1]

**5. Gain eternal perspective: Death is sweet to those who die
in the Lord.** All men must die. Death is an essential element of the
eternal plan of salvation, for it is also birth into the next phase of
man's probationary existence, the spirit world. For the righteous,
it constitutes entrance into Paradise, where man can progress more
rapidly than in mortality, and where he will experience greater joy
than here on earth. Yes, man should make it his goal to live his
mortal life well and fulfill his life's mission with honor, but his
more advanced goal is to leave this "frail existence" and to partake
of the increased blessings available in the spirit world.

As the time approaches for the earth to end its temporal
existence, God will increase the pace of entrance into the next
phase of life, sweeping millions of mortals, both righteous[2] and
wicked, into the spirit existence through the varied judgments of
the last days. For the righteous, death will be a blessing and a
much-desired release from sorrow and tribulation as these events
occur. The wicked will also seek death, but will be without hope
and will fear it.[3]

The saints can bless and prepare themselves by learning about
death and life after death. Joseph Smith taught that "it is important that we should understand...our departure hence...and *it is a
subject we ought to study more than any other.*"[4]

Concerning those who die, the Lord has revealed that

> ...*If they die they shall die unto me, and if they live they shall live
> unto me.*
>
> Thou shalt live together in love, insomuch that thou shalt weep for
> the loss of them that die, and more especially for those that have not
> hope of a glorious resurrection.

---

1. D & C 122:7-8. See verses 1-7.
2. The belief that the righteous will be completely spared from the judgments of the last
   days is incorrect, and in direct contradiction to dozens of scriptural passages. God
   alluded to the death of many of the righteous when he revealed that "the day of my
   visitation cometh speedily, in an hour when ye think not of; and where shall be the
   safety of my people, and refuge for those *who shall be left of them?*" (D & C 124:10.)
3. Rev. 9:6. See also Morm. 2:13-15; 6:7.
4. *HC* 6:50. October 9, 1843.

And it shall come to pass that *those that die in me shall not taste of death, for it shall be sweet unto them;*
And they that die not in me, wo unto them, for their death is bitter.[1]

God has promised that

...All they who suffer persecution for my name, and endure in faith, though they are called to lay down their lives for my sake yet they shall partake of all this glory.
Wherefore, *fear not even unto death;* for in this world your joy is not full, but in me your joy is full.
Therefore, *care not for the body, neither the life of the body; but care for the soul, and for the life of the soul.*
And seek the face of the Lord always, that in patience ye may possess your souls, and ye shall have eternal life.[2]

His instruction has been to

Let no man be afraid to lay down his life for my sake; for whoso layeth down his life for my sake shall find it again.
And whoso is not willing to lay down his life for my sake is not my disciple.[3]

6. **Gain eternal perspective: There must be a transition to Christ's millennial kingdom.** While the prospect of upheaval and chaos in America is extremely unpleasant to contemplate, yet the realization that it will serve as the transition to the Savior's personal rule on earth places it in the necessary perspective. Jesus has revealed,

Wherefore, hear my voice and follow me, and *you shall be a free people, and ye shall have no laws but my laws when I come,* for I am your lawgiver, and what can stay my hand?[4]

His promise is that "I will be your ruler when I come; and behold, I come quickly, and ye shall see that my law is kept."[5] Concerning the saints, he has promised that "the Lord shall be in their midst, and his glory shall be upon them, and *he will be their*

---

1. D & C 42:44-47.
2. D & C 101:35-38. See Al. 24:7-27.
3. D & C 103:27-28. See also D & C 101:10-16; 63:2-4, 49-51; 84:80-84; Mt. 6:25-34; 10:38-39; 16:24-27; 3 Ne. 12:30.
4. D & C 38:22.
5. D & C 41:4.

king and their lawgiver."[1] "The Lord, even the Savior, shall stand in the midst of his people, and shall reign over all flesh."[2]

The judgments which will come upon America will serve to cleanse her, eliminating much of the wicked and criminal element which would not abide by the Savior's rule. The ultimate result will be a change from the present telestial level to the blessings of the terrestrial level which the earth will enjoy during the millennium.[3]

7. Gain eternal perspective: The earth is approaching the end of its temporal existence. It is difficult to understand the events of the last days unless those events are viewed in the light of God's eternal plan. The Lord has revealed that the earth only is to exist under present mortal conditions for a very short period, for he has referred to "the seven thousand years of its continuance, or its temporal existence."[4] Sometime in the beginning of the final thousand years, Christ is to come in glory and rule for a millennium in righteousness.[5] The earth will then undergo a dramatic change,[6] passing away[7] and then being recreated, or resurrected, as a celestial earth.[8] It will be removed from its present location and "placed in the cluster of the celestial kingdoms,"[9] and there complete its eternal mission, serving as an everlasting home for exalted, celestialized beings.[10]

---

1. D & C 45:59.
2. D & C 133:25.
3. "The earth will be renewed and receive its paradisiacal glory." (Article of Faith 10)
4. D & C 77:6.
5. D & C 29:11.
6. As Elder Orson Pratt explained,

   Not only will the elements melt with fervent heat, but *the great globe itself will pass away. It will cease to exist as an organized world.* It will cease to exist as one of the worlds that are capable of being inhabited. Fire devours all things, converting the earth into its original elements; it passes away into space.

   But not one particle of the elements which compose the earth will be destroyed or annihilated. They will all exist and be brought together again by a greater organizing power than is known to man. *The earth must be resurrected again,* as well as our bodies; *its elements will be re-united,* and they will be brought together by the power of God's word. (*JD* 18:346-347. February 25, 1877.)
7. D & C 29:26; 88:25-26.
8. D & C 88:18-19.
9. Brigham Young, *JD* 17:117. June 28, 1874.
10. D & C 88:19-20.

Seen from this perspective, mortal existence upon the earth is a transitory experience—only a brief but important interlude in God's eternal plan. Problems of the world today, such as the "population explosion," the danger of exhausting world food and mineral supplies, and similar concerns, take on a different perspective when viewed with the realization that God's plan does not call for this earth to continue as a mortal habitation much longer than another thousand years. We can have confidence in the Lord's indication that "the earth is full, and *there is enough and to spare;* yea, I have prepared all things."[1]

8. Gain eternal perspective: Look forward to the blessings of the millennial era. As the sorrows of last days' tribulation approach, there is comfort in looking past them to the glorious blessings of the millennial era. The revelations teach that *"he that liveth when the Lord shall come, and hath kept the faith, blessed is he."*[2] It will be a time of peace and harmonious living, and God has revealed that *"they shall not hurt nor destroy* in all my holy mountain; for the earth shall be full of the knowledge of the Lord."[3] Satan will be bound,[4] and men "shall *not labour in vain,* nor bring forth for trouble."[5] After the Savior comes "that same *sociality* which exists among us here will exist among us there, only it will be coupled with eternal glory."[6] The Lord has promised that "you shall be a *free people,* and ye shall have no laws but my laws."[7] The great Jehovah has sworn that in that era "I will pour out my *spirit upon all flesh,"*[8] and "in that day when the Lord shall come, he shall *reveal all things."*[9] Indeed, it will be the "time to come in the which nothing shall be withheld."[10] During the millennial era "there shall be *no sorrow because there is no death,"*[11] and "for the space of a thousand years the *earth shall rest."*[12]

Look forward, past the strife and sorrow of the days of chastisement and cleansing. Focus on the joys of the millennial era, live to be worthy to partake of them, and kindle a hope that the glorious day will soon come.

---

1. D & C 104:17.
2. D & C 63:50.
3. Is. 11:9; 65:25.
4. Rev. 20:1-3. See D & C 101:28.
5. Is. 65:23.
6. D & C 130:2.
7. D & C 38:22.
8. Joel 2:28.
9. D & C 101:32.
10. D & C 121:28.
11. D & C 101:29.
12. Moses 7:64.

Spiritual Preparations for Survival

It must be remembered that the cataclysmic events of the last days are God's judgments upon the wicked. He will send them upon men, and the inhabitants of the earth shall *"be made to feel the wrath, and indignation, and chastening hand of an Almighty God"*[1] in *"the day when the wrath of God shall be poured out upon the wicked without measure."*[2]

Man's wickedness will bring the judgments. Individual righteousness is the only valid shield against them. National righteousness is the only deterent that will prevent their being poured out upon the land.

Personal preparedness through righteous living, being obedient to God's commandments, and being attuned to receive guidance from the Holy Ghost hold the key to survival during the troubled times to come. In these areas the Lord has given much counsel in the scriptures.

9. Cleanse yourself from sins which will bring judgments: Repent. Counsel given by revelation has a vital message for God's people today. The Lord has commanded the saints to

> *Cleanse your hearts and your garments, lest the blood of this generation be required at your hands.*
> Be faithful until I come, for I come quickly; and my reward is with me to recompense every man according as his work shall be.[3]

His commandment has been emphatic:

> *...I command you to repent—repent, lest I smite you* by the rod of my mouth, and by my wrath, and by my anger, *and your sufferings be sore*—how sore you know not, how exquisite you know not, yea, how hard to bear you know not.[4]

His warning is that the judgments will extend to every man who fails to cleanse his life:

> *...Surely every man must repent or suffer,* for I, God, am endless.
> Wherefore I revoke not the judgments which I shall pass, but woes shall go forth, weeping, wailing and gnashing of teeth, yea, to those who are found on my left hand.[5]

---

1. D & C 87:6.
2. D & C 1:9.
3. D & C 112:33-34.

4. D & C 19:15.
5. D & C 19:4-5.

The commandment to repent is given especially to the saints, with the admonition, "Wherefore, *let the church repent of their sins,* and I, the Lord, will own them, otherwise they shall be cut off."[1] The unrepentant saints will lack the inspiration and strength of testimony needed to sustain them when the trials come, for the Lord has warned that "he that repents not, from him shall be taken even the light which he has received; for my Spirit shall not always strive with man...."[2] But for those who will repent of all their sins, his promise is that "I will go before you and be your rearward; and I will be in your midst, and you shall not be confounded."[3]

Here, then, is the grand key to survival—those who will not repent will reap God's judgments, but those who will repent will receive God's guidance and protection in the perilous period ahead. But even the repentant must maintain themselves beyond sin, for the Lord has commanded,

> Abide ye in the liberty wherewith ye are made free; *entangle not yourselves in sin, but let your hands be clean, until the Lord comes.*[4]

10. Escape judgments through obedience: Keep God's commandments. Obedience to God's commandments will also provide the avenue for escape from the judgments to come. A revelation warns that

> ...The indignation of the Lord is kindled against their abominations and all their wicked works.
> Nevertheless, *Zion shall escape if she observe to do all things whatsoever I have commanded her.*[5]

While warning of sin, pride, covetousness, and detestable things among the saints, the Lord stressed that repentance and obedience are the keys to escaping his judgments:

> Verily I say unto you, that *I, the Lord, will chasten them and will do whatsoever I list, if they do not repent and observe all things whatsoever I have said unto them.*
> And again I say unto you, *if ye observe to do whatsoever I command you, I, the Lord, will turn away all wrath and indignation* from you, and the gates of hell shall not prevail against you.[6]

---

1. D & C 63:63. See D & C 84:55-59.
2. D & C 1:33.
3. D & C 49:26-27.
4. D & C 88:86.
5. D & C 97:24-25.
6. D & C 98:21-22.

Obedience to every commandment God reveals will be the test which the saints must meet, as the Lord proves them with the trials of the last days:

> ...I give unto you a commandment, that ye shall forsake all evil and cleave unto all good, that *ye shall live by every word which proceedeth forth out of the mouth of God.*
> For he will give unto the faithful line upon line, precept upon precept; and *I will try you and prove you herewith.*
> And whoso layeth down his life in my cause, for my name's sake, shall find it again, even life eternal.[1]

Just as God's guidance is pledged for the repentant, he has promised to shape events for the benefit of the obedient in the last days:

> Keep all the commandments and covenants by which ye are bound; and *I will cause the heavens to shake for your good,* and Satan shall tremble and Zion shall rejoice upon the hills and flourish.[2]

But loss of the faith and the triumph of their enemies await those who fail to render obedience:

> Be diligent in keeping all my commandments, *lest judgments come upon you, and your faith fail you, and your enemies triumph over you.*[3]

11. Be free from the sins of the generation: Sanctify yourselves. Sanctification is the process whereby men "yield their hearts unto God,"[4] so that the Holy Ghost helps them to deny themselves of all ungodliness and thus become holy individuals[5] able to stand spotless before God.[6] Their garments are "washed white through the blood of the Lamb" and sin becomes abhorrent to them.[7]

In the last days context, the Lord has warned that "all those who will not endure chastening, but deny me, cannot be sanctified."[8] Concerning the day of his coming in glory, he has revealed that "the day soon cometh that ye shall see me, and know that I am; for the veil of darkness shall soon be rent, and *he that is not purified shall not abide the day.*[9]

1. D & C 98:11-13. See D & C 45:2, 6.
2. D & C 35:24.
3. D & C 136:42.
4. Hel. 3:35.
5. Moro. 10:32-33.
6. 3 Ne. 27:20.
7. Al. 13:11-12.
8. D & C 101:5.
9. D & C 38:8.

Their being sanctified will enable the saints to be found free from the blood and sins of this wicked generation. The Lord has revealed,

> *Behold, I will hasten my work in its time.*
> And I give unto you, who are the first laborers in this last kingdom, a commandment that you assemble yourselves together, and organize yourselves, and prepare yourselves, and *sanctify yourselves; yea, purify your hearts, and cleanse your hands and your feet before me, that I may make you clean;*
> *That I may testify unto your Father, and your God, and my God, that you are clean from the blood of this wicked generation;...*[1]

The sanctification process causes an actual change and renewing of the body.[2] John the Revelator has told of 144,000 men who will be called from the tribes of Israel and "sealed...in their foreheads."[3] These men will labor during the judgments of the last days to bring converts into the church.[4] As Elder Orson Pratt explained, God "will purify their bodies until they shall be quickened, and renewed and strengthened, and they will be partially changed.... This will prepare them for further ministrations among the nations of the earth,...they can stand forth in the midst of these desolations and plagues and not be overcome by them."[5]

Attaining sanctification, then, will shield the saints from the judgments, allow them to be accounted free from the blood and sins of the generations, and prepare them to receive the full eternal benefits of the Lord's atoning sacrifice.

12. Prepare Spiritually: Be guided by the Holy Ghost. Ability to receive inspiration and guidance of the Spirit will be necessary for survival of the saints during the judgments of the last days. The Lord has revealed that

> ...At that day, when I shall come in my glory, shall the parable be fulfilled which I spake concerning the ten virgins.
> *For they that are wise and have received the truth, and have taken the Holy Spirit for their guide, and have not been deceived*—verily I say

---

1. D & C 88:73-75. See verses 85, 138; 109:42; 112:33.
2. See D & C 84:33; 88:67-68.
3. Rev. 7:3.
4. For more detailed information on the 144,000 see the author's book, *Prophecy—Key to the Future,* pp. 121-125, 141-142.
5. *JD* 15:365-366. March 9, 1873.

unto you they shall not be hewn down and cast into the fire, but shall abide the day.[1]

Recognizing promptings of approaching danger; receiving guidance on methods of obtaining food and other necessary items; being directed in where to live and travel; discerning between friends and enemies, truth and error, true and false prophets—all these abilities will be indispensible when the period of "the desolation of abomination" begins. But being continually receptive to the Spirit does not come easily. It requires a conditioning of the mind and will—a humbling and cleansing of the self:

> Let him that is ignorant *learn wisdom by humbling himself and calling upon the Lord his God*, that his eyes may be opened that he may see, and his ears opened that he may hear;
> *For my Spirit is sent forth into the world to enlighten the humble and contrite, and to the condemnation of the ungodly.*[2]

"Ye receive the Spirit through prayer,"[3] drawing near unto God so that he in turn draws near unto you.[4] The power of the Holy Spirit is then bestowed by God "on those who love him, and purify themselves before him."[5] There is the need to develop a relationship of faith and trust in the promptings which come:

> *...Put your trust in that Spirit which leadeth to do good*—yea, to do justly, to walk humbly, to judge righteously; and this is my Spirit.
> Verily, verily, I say unto you, *I will impart unto you of my Spirit, which shall enlighten your mind, which shall fill your soul with joy;*
> *And then shall ye know, or by this shall you know, all things whatsoever you desire of me*, which are pertaining unto things of righteousness, in faith believing in me that you shall receive.[6]

The Holy Ghost is a comforter,[7] who will teach and bring necessary things to remembrance.[8] He will testify of the Christ,[9] guide into all truth,[10] and will reveal things to come[11]—all of which are blessings which will be sorely needed by the saints during the era of future strife and chaos.

---

1. D & C 45:56-57.
2. D & C 136:32-33.
3. D & C 63:64. See 14:8.
4. D & C 88:63-65.
5. D & C 76:116.
6. D & C 11:12-14.

7. Jn. 14:26.
8. *Ibid.*
9. Jn. 15:26.
10. Jn. 16:13.
11. *Ibid.*

13. Recognize last days events: Watch for signs of the times.
The Lord instructed his people to be alert to signs that prophesied
events are about to take place. After giving his great prophecy of
last days events to his disciples on the Mount of Olives, he told
them,

> Now learn a parable of the fig tree; when his branch is yet tender,
> and putteth forth leaves, ye know that summer is nigh:
>
> So likewise ye, when ye shall see all these things, know that it is
> near, even at the doors.[1]

One of the identifying characteristics of those who fear and
serve the Lord is their awareness of the signs of the times. As the
Savior observed,

> ...He that feareth me shall be looking forth for the great day of the
> Lord to come, *even for the signs of the coming of the Son of Man....*
> And he that watches not for me shall be cut off.[2]

An understanding of the signs of the times is promised to the
saints:

> And he that believeth shall be blest with signs following, even as it
> is written.
>
> *And unto you it shall be given to know the signs of the times, and
> the signs of the coming of the Son of Man;...*[3]

The Lord's instruction is to

> Gird up your loins and be watchful and be sober, *looking forth for
> the coming of the Son of Man,* for he cometh in an hour you think not.[4]

The purposes of knowing the prophesied signs of the times,
and then being aware of their fulfillment as the events transpire,
are fourfold. First, that knowledge prevents deception and confusion:

> Wherefore, *be not deceived,* but continue in steadfastness, looking
> forth for the heavens to be shaken, and the earth to tremble and to reel
> to and fro as a drunken man, and for the valleys to be exalted, and for

---

1. Mt. 24:32-33. See D & C 35:16.
2. D & C 45:39, 44.
3. D & C 68:10-11.
4. D & C 61:38.

the mountains to be made low, and for the rough places to become smooth—[1]

Second, observing the fulfillment of the signs of the times reminds the saints of their need to maintain personal worthiness:

>...*Take heed to yourselves,* lest at any time your hearts be overcharged with surfeiting, and drunkenness, and cares of this life, and so that day come upon you unawares.
>
>For as a snare shall it come on all them that dwell on the face of the whole earth.
>
>*Watch ye therefore, and pray always, that ye may be accounted worthy to escape all these things that shall come to pass, and to stand before the Son of Man.*[2]

Third, knowing the prophesied events and the order in which they will transpire allows one to prepare for them and to accept them when they take place. The Lord, speaking of the tribulations of the last days, has told the saints to "remember this, *which I tell you before,* that you may lay it to heart, and *receive that which is to follow.*"[3]

Finally, knowing the prophecies and recognizing the signs of the times allows the saints to bear witness of God's hand in future events:

>Behold, verily I say unto you, for this cause I have sent you—that you might be obedient, and *that your hearts might be prepared to bear testimony of the things which are to come;...*[4]

The author has observed "the ostrich syndrome" among the saints from time to time. There are those who say "I don't want to know about the prophecies of last days—they frighten me." Others have said, "The prophecies are negative in their approach. We should 'think positive'—let's only talk about happy things." Their philosophies are not the Lord's way, and are in direct opposition to his oft-repeated instructions. They neither prepare themselves, nor fulfill the commandments that they should warn and prepare others. They would do well to heed the Lord's warning that "*he that watches not for me shall be cut off.*"[5]

---

1. D & C 49:23.
2. Lk. 21:34-36. See also Mt. 24:42; 25:13; Mk. 13:35-37; Lk. 12:37-40; Eph. 6:18; 1 Thess. 5:6; 1 Pet. 4:7; Rev. 16:15.
3. D & C 58:5. See D & C 106:4-5.
4. D & C 58:6.
5. D & C 45:44.

14. Teach doctrines of the last days: Seek knowledge for protection. A major element in the spiritual preparation of the saints is the necessity of their being properly informed concerning the prophecies of the last days. The Lord has emphasized that this people need to understand what is prophesied to come to pass, and they need to be able to discern the signs of the times by recognizing the preparations for these events among the nations of the earth. This instruction was given by revealed commandment:

> *And I give unto you a commandment that you shall teach one another the doctrine of the kingdom.*
> Teach ye diligently and my grace shall attend you, that you may be instructed more perfectly in *theory,* in *principle,* in *doctrine,* in the *law of the gospel,* in *all things that pertain unto the kingdom of God,* that are expedient for you to understand;
> Of things both in heaven and in the earth, and under the earth; *things which have been, things which are, things which must shortly come to pass; things which are at home, things which are abroad; the wars and the perplexities of the nations, and the judgments which are on the land; and a knowledge also of countries and of kingdoms—*
> *That ye may be prepared in all things* when I shall send you again to magnify the calling whereunto I have called you, and the mission with which I have commissioned you.[1]

Not only are the saints commanded to teach each other about the things which are to come to pass, they are also commanded to personally "treasure up wisdom" to protect themselves against the wickedness of men in the last days:

> And again, I say unto you that the *enemy in the secret chambers seeketh your lives.*
> Ye hear of wars in far countries, and you say that there will soon be great wars in far countries, but ye know not the hearts of men in your own land.
> I tell you these things because of your prayers; wherefore, *treasure up wisdom in your bosoms, lest the wickedness of men reveal these things unto you by their wickedness,* in a manner which shall speak in your ears with a voice louder than that which shall shake the earth; but *if ye are prepared ye shall not fear.*
> And that ye might *escape the power of the enemy, and be gathered unto me a righteous people,* without spot and blameless—[2]

15. Prepare the saints for the hour of judgment: Warn your neighbor. After commanding the saints to teach one another about

---

1. D & C 88:77-80. See also D & C 88:118; 97:12-14.
2. D & C 38:28-31.

"things which must shortly come to pass" and about the "judgments which are on the land,"[1] the Lord specified the warning duty required of all his people:

> Behold, I sent you out to *testify and warn the people*, and *it becometh every man who hath been warned to warn his neighbor.*[2]

The context of this passage clearly indicates that the warning spoken of by the Savior is not merely the preaching of general gospel principles. That warning is

> *...to prepare the saints for the hour of judgment which is to come;* that their souls may *escape the wrath of God, the desolation of abomination* which awaits the wicked, both in this world and in the world to come.[3]

In the dedicatory prayer for the Kirtland Temple, which was given to the Prophet Joseph Smith by revelation, deep concern is expressed for the need to prepare the saints against coming judgments:

> Put upon thy servants the testimony of the covenant, that when they go out and proclaim thy word they may seal up the law, and *prepare the hearts of thy saints for all those judgments thou art about to send,* in thy wrath, upon the inhabitants of the earth, because of their transgressions, *that thy people may not faint in the day of trouble.*[4]

And also:

> We know that thou hast spoken by the mouth of thy prophets terrible things concerning the wicked, in the last days—that thou wilt pour out thy judgments, without measure;
> Therefore, O Lord, *deliver thy people from the calamity of the wicked;* enable thy servants to seal up the law, and bind up the testimony, that *they may be prepared against the day of burning.*[5]

The Lord has commanded the saints repeatedly to

> *Prepare ye, prepare ye for that which is to come,* for the Lord is nigh;
> And the anger of the Lord is kindled, and his sword is bathed in heaven, and it shall fall upon the inhabitants of the earth.[6]

---

1. See again D & C 88:79.
2. D & C 88:81.
3. D & C 88:84-85.
4. D & C 109:38.
5. D & C 109:45-46.
6. D & C 1:12-13. See also D & C 31:8; 33:10; 65:1-3; 85:3; 88:92; 133:4-5, 10, 19.

He has told them that

> ...I give unto you a commandment, that *every man*, both elder, priest, teacher, and also member, go to with his might, with the labor of his hands, *to prepare and accomplish the things which I have commanded.*
> *And let your preaching be the warning voice, every man to his neighbor,* in mildness and in meekness.[1]

The commandment of the Lord, then, is that the saints admonish and warn one another, helping each other to prepare for the difficult times to come. This, obviously, is the motive for this book.

16. Preach repentance to non-members: Warn of coming judgments. The Lord has commanded that warning of coming judgments be a major part of the missionary message to the world at large in the last days. Two messages, repentance and the warning of coming judgments, are to go hand in hand as the major themes of missionary labor. The Lord told the elders, for instance, *"Behold, I sent you out to reprove the world of all their unrighteous deeds, and to teach them of a judgment which is to come."*[2] He commanded that all the church should preach that two-fold message:

> And verily I say unto you, the rest of my servants, go ye forth as your circumstances shall permit, in your several callings, unto the great and notable cities and villages, *reproving the world in righteousness of all their unrighteous and ungodly deeds, setting forth clearly and understandingly the desolation of abomination in the last days.*[3]

The Lord has instructed those laboring in the missionary effort to "open your mouths and they shall be filled, saying: *Repent, repent, and prepare ye the way of the Lord,* and make his paths straight; for the kingdom of heaven is at hand;..."[4] Another revelation instructs those who are called to preach the gospel to

> ...*Cry repentance* unto a crooked and perverse generation, *preparing the way of the Lord* for his second coming.
> For behold, verily, verily, I say unto you, the time is soon at hand that I shall come in a cloud with power and great glory.

---

1. D & C 38:40-41.
2. D & C 84:87.
3. D & C 84:117. The same dual message, of calling to repentance and prophesying of future judgments, characterized the work even in the days of Enoch. See Moses 6:27.
4. D & C 33:10.

And it shall be a great day at the time of my coming, for all nations shall tremble.

But before that great day shall come, the sun shall be darkened, and the moon be turned into blood; and the stars shall refuse their shining, and some shall fall, and *great destructions await the wicked.*

Wherefore, *lift up your voice and spare not,* for the Lord God hath spoken; therefore *prophesy,* and it shall be given by the power of the Holy Ghost.[1]

And also:

Lift up your voices and spare not. *Call upon the nations to repent,* both old and young, both bond and free, *saying: Prepare yourselves for the great day of the Lord;*

For if I, who am a man, do lift up my voice and call upon you to repent, and ye hate me, what will ye say when the day cometh when the thunders shall utter their voices from the ends of the earth, speaking to the ears of all that live, saying—Repent, and prepare for the great day of the Lord?[2]

Thus the two-fold message of latter-day missionaries is clearly set forth by the Lord. They are to call to repentance, and prepare the people for the Lord's coming by warning of the judgments of the last days.

Warning of future events is required of those who are obedient to the Lord, and is not to be omitted from the missionary message:

Behold, verily I say unto you, for this cause I have sent you, that you might *be obedient,* and that your hearts might be prepared *to bear testimony of the things which are to come;...*[3]

And that requirement extends to "every man":

Wherefore, seeing that I, the Lord, have decreed all these things upon the face of the earth, I will that my saints should be assembled upon the land of Zion;

And that *every man* should take righteousness in his hands and faithfulness upon his loins, and *lift a warning voice unto the inhabitants of the earth;* and declare both by word and by flight that desolation shall come upon the wicked.[4]

17. Bind the law and seal the testimony: Testify against the wicked. The Lord has revealed that this wicked generation has

---

1. D & C 34:6-10.   3. D & C 58:6.
2. D & C 43:20-21.   4. D & C 63:36-37.

ripened in iniquity until it is now *"white already to be burned."*[1]
It is now the eleventh hour, and the last time missionaries will be
called:

> ...Ye are called to lift up your voices as with the sound of a trump, to
> *declare my gospel unto a crooked and perverse generation.*
> For behold, the field is white already to harvest; and it is the *eleventh
> hour,* and the *last time* that I shall call laborers into my vineyard.
> *And my vineyard has become corrupted every whit; and there is none
> which doeth good save it be a few;* and they err in many instances be-
> cause of priestcrafts, all having corrupt minds.[2]

This "crooked and perverse generation"[3] has become so
wicked the Lord is withholding his spirit from the inhabitants of
the earth.[4] The saints have been instructed to

> ...Watch, for the adversary spreadeth his dominions, and darkness reign-
> eth;
> And the anger of God kindleth against the inhabitants of the earth;
> *and none doeth good, for all have gone out of the way.*[5]

Concerning the rest of the world besides the saints, the Lord has
revealed that

> *...All flesh is corrupted before me; and the powers of darkness prevail
> upon the earth,* among the children of men, in the presence of all the
> hosts of heaven—
> Which causeth silence to reign, and all eternity is pained, and *the
> angels are waiting the great command to reap down the earth,* to gather
> the tares that they may be burned; and, behold, *the enemy is combined.*[6]

God has decreed that "this gospel of the kingdom shall be
preached in all the world *for a witness unto all nations;* and then
shall the end come."[7] The Lord has said that the missionaries are
"called to prune my vineyard with a *mighty pruning,* yea, even for
the last time."[8] This witness, or "pruning," will serve to convert
and gather out the righteous who remain, but it will also condemn
the wicked. Speaking of those who will have believed on his words
and will have been born again, the Lord said, "Their testimony
shall also go forth *unto the condemnation of this generation* if
they harden their hearts against them."[9]

---

1. D & C 31:4.
2. D & C 33:2-4.
3. D & C 34:6.
4. D & C 63:32.
5. D & C 82:5-6.

6. D & C 38:11-12.
7. Mt. 24:14.
8. D & C 24:19.
9. D & C 5:18.

The Lord's servants are to seal up the righteous to partake of the blessings of eternal life and to be protected against Satan's power in the last days.[1] They have a similar responsibility to seal up the wicked unto judgment and condemnation. A revelation from the Savior states that

>...They who go forth, bearing these tidings unto the inhabitants of the earth, *to them is power given to seal both on earth and in heaven, the unbelieving and rebellious;*
>
>Yea, verily, *to seal them up unto the day when the wrath of God shall be poured out upon the wicked without measure—*[2]

This "sealing up" process is a fundamental aspect of the labor of the missionaries in the last days. The Lord has commanded,

>...Tarry ye, and labor diligently, that you may be perfected in your ministry to go forth among the Gentiles for the last time, as many as the mouth of the Lord shall name, *to bind up the law and seal up the testimony,...*[3]

Then the Lord's answer to the wicked at the last day shall be that they have been sealed up unto darkness by the Lord's servants:

>Behold, and lo, there are none to deliver you; for ye obeyed not my voice when I called to you out of the heavens; ye believed not my servants, and when they were sent unto you ye received them not.
>
>Wherefore, *they sealed up the testimony and bound up the law,* and ye were delivered over unto darkness.[4]

Thus the Lord's servants have been commanded to leave a witness against those who reject them by shaking off the dust from their feet,[5] and they eventually stand as witnesses of the house, village or city which cast them out.[6] The Lord has said, concerning enemies who come against the saints to drive them out,

>*...Ye shall curse them;*
>
>*And whomsoever ye curse, I will curse, and ye shall avenge me of mine enemies.*
>
>And my presence shall be with you even in avenging me of mine enemies, unto the third and fourth generation of them that hate me.[7]

---

1. See D & C 68:11-12; 109:38; 124:124; 131:5.
2. D & C 1:8-9. See D & C 124:93; 128:8-11.
3. D & C 88:84.
4. D & C 133:71-72.
5. D & C 24:15-17; 60:15; 99:4-5.
6. D & C 75:18-22; 84:92-97.
7. D & C 103:24-26.

Bearing testimony against the wicked is an awesome responsibility, and one not to be taken lightly, nor used indiscriminately without careful restraint! Yet it is a duty commanded of God, and an integral part of his plan. It is necessary in the last days, just as it was in Alma's time[1] and in the era of the New Testament church.[2] As the gap between righteousness and iniquity widens, the necessity for testimony against the wicked will rapidly increase.

18. Go ye out from Babylon: Be separate from the wicked. The Lord has commanded, "Prepare ye, prepare ye, O my people,"[3] and then has told the saints to *"go ye out from Babylon. Be ye clean that bear the vessels of the Lord."*[4] In another revelation his counsel is to *"go ye out from among the wicked. Save yourselves."*[5] Another warning proclaims the Lord's message that "all the proud and they that do wickedly shall be as stubble; and I will burn them up, for I am the Lord of Hosts; and *I will not spare any that remain in Babylon."*[6] The Lord's instruction has been given to *"Go ye out from among the nations, even from Babylon, from the midst of wickedness, which is spiritual Babylon."*[7]

That saint who wishes to be spiritually and temporally prepared would do well to examine the environment in which he lives and works. He should evaluate his situation, prayerfully assessing whether his surroundings and associates are conducive to his living the gospel, or whether his environment is leading him and his family away from that which is righteous and good. It would be to his benefit, also, to evaluate what the situation would be if difficult conditions were to arise such as severe food shortages, international war or internal conflict, or persecution of the Church. In such extreme situations, would he be able to continue in his present surroundings, or would he be subjected to severe pressures, and perhaps even have to "take his sword against his neighbor"[8] in defense of his family, his home, his supplies, and his liberty? Every Latter-day Saint who is in tune with the Holy Spirit is entitled to revealed guidance concerning where he should work and reside. Such promptings come to many. Indeed, over the past decade the author has conversed with numerous individuals who had moved to new environments because of personal inspiration which they have received.

1. Al. 14:11.
2. Lk. 11:49-51.
3. D & C 133:4.
4. D & C 133:5.

5. D & C 38:42.
6. D & C 64:24.
7. D & C 133:14.
8. D & C 45:68.

The present activity and direction of the Church, however, should be considered when making a decision concerning where to live. In this day of "lengthened stride" towards missionary work, the gospel message is being taught world-wide. The place where the saints are most needed is in the outlying stakes and missions, where they can be most actively involved with the rapid growth, rather than being clustered in the center of the Church. No general "gathering" call has been given, and it still appears *necessary that ye should remain for the present time in your places of abode*, as it shall be suitable to your circumstances."[1] It is still a time of preparation prior to the gathering, but a time to assist the saints and to *"strengthen them and prepare them* against the time when they shall be gathered."[2]

Even at the height of the future difficulties, when the Church will be the subject of intense persecution, the saints will still be scattered throughout the world. In his vision of that future era, Nephi saw that "the church of the Lamb, who were the saints of God, were also *upon all the face of the earth;...*"[3]

The scriptures indicate that there will be two times, and types, of gathering. The first will be to various places of refuge among the stakes of Zion, as the nation endures the agonies of world war and internal conflict. Then, after the Missouri area has been swept clean, the New Jerusalem will be built. The scriptures reveal that there will be a general assemblying to that area. No advantage is to be gained by undirected moves which are out of chronological synchronization with these periods. To move to the New Jerusalem area, prior to its cleansing, for instance, could be disasterous.

In the first gathering period, the saints will have need to assemble in various places of refuge   throughout the Americas, the "land of Zion,"[4] among the stakes:

---

1. D & C 48:1.
2. D & C 31:8.
3. 1 Ne. 14:12. Nephi added, however, that "their dominions upon the face of the earth were small, because of the wickedness of the great whore whom I saw." *(Ibid.)*
4. In this passage the term "Zion" appears to be used in the broad sense, as expressed by Joseph Smith in the April, 1844 conference: ..."I will make a proclamation that will cover a broader ground. *The whole of America is Zion itself from north to south,* and is described by the prophets, who declare that it is the Zion where the mountain of the Lord should be, and that it should be in the center of the land." *(HC* 6:318-319. April 8, 1844.)

...That the gathering together upon *the land of Zion, and upon her stakes, may be for a defense, and for a refuge from the storm,* and from wrath when it shall be poured out without mixture upon the whole earth.[1]

The Lord speaks of *"Zion, and in her stakes, and in Jerusalem"* as "those places which I have appointed for refuge."[2] He revealed that his will is that the saints "gather together, and stand in holy places."[3] The Savior says that as the overflowing scourge of sickness is poured out, "My disciples shall stand in holy places, and shall not be moved."[4] The Lord has cautioned that this gathering should be accomplished *"not in haste, lest there should be confusion, which bringeth pestilence."*[5] His caution to the saints is to "let not your gathering be in haste, nor by flight; but *let all things be prepared before you."*[6] It appears that the saints will need to be alert to this approaching time of gathering to places of refuge, and not tarry or procrastinate when the need arises.

A prophetic statement made by President Heber C. Kimball seems to indicate that the separation, or "sifting time," will even involve the saints of the Utah area. In 1856 he said,

> We think we are secure here in the chambers of the everlasting hills, where we can close those few doors of the canyons against mobs and persecutors, the wicked and the vile, who have always beset us with violence and robbery, but I want to say to you, my brethren, the time is coming when *we will be mixed up in these now peaceful valleys to that extent that it will be difficult to tell the face of a Saint from the face of an enemy to the people of God. Then, brethren, look out for the great sieve, for there will be a great sifting time, and many will fall;* for I say unto you there is a *test,* a *TEST,* a TEST coming, and who will be able to stand?[7]

The scriptures also speak of a second gathering, a later assembling of the saints, at the site of the New Jerusalem in Missouri:

---

1. D & C 115:6.
2. D & C 124:36.
3. D & C 101:22. Verses 20-22 allude to the stakes as being the "holy places." See also verses 64-68.
4. D & C 45:32. See 87:8.
5. D & C 63:24.
6. D & C 101:68.
7. Orson F. Whitney, *Life of Heber C. Kimball* (Salt Lake City, Utah: Bookcraft, 1967), p. 446. This statement was preserved by Elder Edward Stevenson. President A.F. McDonald recorded, concerning Heber C. Kimball, that "he clearly foreshadowed the time of trial the Saints are now passing through, *and to a period still before us. He often used the language, 'A test, a test is coming.'* " (*Ibid.* p. 447.)

...The decree hath gone forth from the Father that they shall be gathered in unto *one place upon the face of this land,* to prepare their hearts and be prepared in all things against the day when *tribulation and desolation are sent forth upon the wicked.*[1]

The Lord has revealed his desire "that my covenant people may be *gathered in one* in that day when I shall come to my temple."[2] He described the New Jerusalem as a "city of refuge, a place of safety for the saints of the Most High God,"[3] and said that

...It shall come to pass among the wicked, that *every man that will not take his sword against his neighbor must needs flee unto Zion for safety.*

And there shall be gathered unto it out of every nation under heaven; and it shall be the only people that shall not be at war one with another.[4]

Yet even in that day, when world-wide conflict will make it imperative that the saints be "gathered in one," there will still be those who will have been "commanded to tarry"[5] who will be scattered throughout the world.[6]

To be prepared to gather to appropriate places of refuge as the difficulties come upon the world will require individual alertness to personal promptings and responsiveness to Church directions, plus adequate preparation for mobility, coupled with the realization that many saints will find it necessary to *"declare both by word and by flight that desolation shall come upon the wicked."*[7] It will be necessary to grasp and accept the implications of a separation of the obedient from the disobedient and unjust. It will also place tremendous responsibility upon Church authorities to properly prepare the saints and to help them develop adequate places of refuge, and also to be sufficiently responsive to divine guidance that they can give proper and timely directives in a time when many lives are at stake and the potential for human suffering is enormous.

19. Seek divine strength, guidance and protection: Pray always. There is tremendous strength and power gained through effective

---

1. D & C 29:8.
2. D & C 42:36.
3. D & C 45:66.
4. D & C 45:68-69.
5. D & C 133:4.
6. See again 1 Ne. 14:12. Also *Prophecy—Key to the Future,* pp. 90-91.
7. D & C 63:37.

prayer and the Lord has commanded that his people utilize that strength for their own benefit during the difficult events of the last days.

Elder Heber C. Kimball spoke of the importance of each individual being personally receptive to divine guidance and possessing a firm testimony in connection with the events of the last days. He said,

> This Church has before it many close places through which it will have to pass before the work of God is crowned with victory. To meet the difficulties that are coming, *it will be necessary for you to have a knowledge of the truth of this work for yourselves. The difficulties will be of such a character that the man or woman who does not possess this personal knowledge or witness will fall.* If you have not got the testimony, live right and call upon the Lord and cease not till you obtain it. If you do not you will not stand.
>
> Remember these sayings, for many of you will live to see them fulfilled. *The time will come when no man nor woman will be able to endure on borrowed light. Each will have to be guided by the light within himself. If you do not have it, how can you stand?* Do you believe it?...
>
> *You will have all the persecution you want and more too,* and all the opportunity to show your integrity to God and truth that you could desire.[1]

On another occasion he remarked, *"Unless a man knew that Jesus was the Christ, he could not stand in this Church.* He said

---

1. Orson F. Whitney, *Life of Heber C. Kimball, op. cit.,* pp. 449-450, 451. In this same discourse, delivered in 1867, he said:

> You have the First Presidency, from whom you can get counsel to guide you, and you rely on them. The time will come when they will not be with you. Why? Because *they will have to flee and hide up to keep out of the hands of their enemies.* You have the Twelve now. You will not always have them, for *they too will be hunted and will have to keep out of the way of their enemies.* You have other men to whom you look for counsel and advice. Many of them will not be amongst you, for the same reason. *You will be left to the light within yourselves. If you don't have it you will not stand; therefore seek for the testimony of Jesus and cleave to it, that when the trying time comes you may not stumble and fall.* (*Ibid.,* p. 450.)

The saints endured this type of experience during the anti-Mormon persecutions of the 1880's. Whether a similar situation will occur in connection with the persecutions prophesied for the future remains to be seen. The fulfillment of Heber C. Kimball's prophecy that *"the time would come when the government would stop the Saints from holding meetings. When this was done the Lord would pour out His judgments,"* (*Ibid.,* p. 442) has not yet been realized. Does it imply future persecution from Governmental sources, and foreshadow a similar situation to the 1880's period?

that the Lord would allow all manner of abominations to come to Zion, in order to purify His people."[1]

The Savior has commanded that Divine supplication be made for many things, but foremost is individual prayer for protection and strength so that one can endure till Christ comes. The revealed instruction has been given to *"Pray always that you enter not into temptation,* that you may abide the day of his coming, whether in life or in death."[2] A similar revelation conveyed the Savior's admonition to *"Pray always, that ye may not faint, until I come. Behold, and lo, I will come quickly, and receive you unto myself."*[3]

Diligent obedience is required if the saints are to be able to rely on prayer to assist them when troubled times come. Said the Lord concerning earlier saints,

> They were slow to hearken unto the voice of the Lord their God; therefore, the *Lord their God is slow to hearken unto their prayers, to answer them in the day of their trouble.*[4]

The Lord had delivered the same warning to the people of King Noah in Book of Mormon times:

> ...Except this people repent and turn unto the Lord their God, they shall be brought into bondage; and none shall deliver them, except it be the Lord the Almighty God.
>
> Yea, and it shall come to pass that *when they shall cry unto me I will be slow to hear their cries; yea, and I will suffer them that they be smitten by their enemies.*
>
> And except they repent in sackcloth and ashes, and cry mightily to the Lord their God, *I will not hear their prayers, neither will I deliver them out of their afflictions;...*[5]

Truly no course but righteous obedience can safely be followed in the perilous times to come.

Another scriptural warning speaks of prayer being made ineffective because of unwillingness to share with the needy. As the shortages and famines of the last days occur, this may become a matter of serious import, affecting both the temporal and spiritual salvation of many:

---

1. *Ibid.,* p. 441. This statement was made in 1856.
2. D & C 61:39.
3. D & C 88:126.
4. D & C 101:7.
5. Mos. 11:23-25. See also Mos. 7:29, 33; 9:3, 17-18; 21:14-15.

*...If ye turn away the needy, and the naked, and visit not the sick and afflicted, and impart of your substance, if ye have, to those who stand in need—*I say unto you, if ye do not any of these things, behold, *your prayer is vain, and availeth you nothing,* and ye are as hypocrites who do deny the faith.[1]

The saints would do well to pray for the nation and its leaders, seeking that it might follow a course of righteousness, and making supplication that impending judgments be delayed until the Lord's work of gleaning the righteous is accomplished. As in Book of Mormon times, such prayers can delay the judgments, a process which may presently be happening:

Yea, and I say unto you that *if it were not for the prayers of the righteous, who are now in the land, that ye would even now be visited with utter destruction;* yet it would not be by flood as were the people in the days of Noah, but it would be by famine, and by pestilence, and the sword.

But it is by the prayers of the righteous that ye are spared; now therefore, if ye will *cast out the righteous from among you then will not the Lord stay his hand;* but in his fierce anger he will come out against you; then ye shall be smitten by famine, and by pestilence, and by the sword; and the time is soon at hand except ye repent.[2]

Yet prayer alone cannot save the nations—only their repentance and acceptance of the gospel can avert the judgments. The Lord has said,

Behold, verily, verily, I say unto you, that the people in Ohio call upon me in much faith, *thinking I will stay my hand in judgment upon the nations, but I cannot deny my word.*

Wherefore lay to with your might and call faithful laborers into my vineyard, that it may be pruned for the last time.

And inasmuch as they do repent and receive the fulness of my gospel, and become sanctified, I will stay mine hand in judgment.[3]

Like the prophets and disciples of old, the saints should seek to "leave a blessing upon this land in their prayers."[4] Yet there

---

1. Al. 34:28.
2. Al. 10:22-23. Concerning the time in the last days when the Lord will "in his fury vex the nation," the Lord has instructed the saints to "Pray ye, therefore, *that their ears may be opened unto your cries,* that I may be merciful unto them, that these things may not come upon them." (D & C 101:92.)
3. D & C 39:16-18.
4. See D & C 10:46-52.

will come a time, when the persecution against the saints becomes intense, that they may be

> Calling upon the name of the Lord day and night, saying: *O that thou wouldst rend the heavens*, that thou wouldst come down, that the mountains might flow down at thy presence....
> O Lord, *thou shalt come down to make thy name known to thine adversaries*, and all nations shall tremble at thy presence—
> When thou doest terrible things,...[1]

20. Prepare for return of the united order: Be ready to share. With the strong prophetic warnings concerning future famine which have been given, there is reason to ponder how the needs of large portions of the population can be met. Surely there is need for the saints to "warn their neighbor," encouraging those around them to anticipate the possibility of future shortages. But the question "Must I share in a time of extreme need?" often arises.

The third world war and internal conflict within the United States will serve as a transition period, in preparation for the return of the saints to establish the New Jerusalem. The Lord has revealed that by the time of that return, the saints must again be living the united order, for that unity is a

> ...Union required by the law of the celestial kingdom;
> And *Zion cannot be built up unless it is by the principles of the law of the celestial kingdom;* otherwise I cannot receive her unto myself.[2]

Just how, and when, the principle of consecration under the united order is to be reinstated is not known by the author, but it is obvious that a major need may arise if famine and extreme shortages come upon the saints. Such a scenario might set the stage, creating sufficient need that the saints might overcome the obstacle of selfishness which prevented the united order from becoming their way of life in the past.[3]

The Lord has said that the united order is to be "for the benefit of my church, and *for the salvation of men until I come*."[4] While speaking of the united order, he revealed that it was to serve to make the church independent in the time of tribulation:

---

1. D & C 133:40, 42-43. See Al. 33:10; D & C 109:50-52.
2. D & C 105:4-5.
3. See D & C 105:1-10.
4. D & C 104:1.

Behold, this is the preparation wherewith I prepare you, and the foundation, and the ensample which I give unto you, whereby you may accomplish the commandments which are given you;

That through my providence, *notwithstanding the tribulation which shall descend upon you, that the church may stand independent* above all other creatures beneath the celestial world;...[1]

And he also said,

...*It is my purpose to provide for my saints,* for all things are mine.

But it must needs be done in mine own way; and behold *this is the way that I, the Lord, have decreed to provide for my saints,*...[2]

Sometime in the future, then, the saints can expect the Lord to again command them, saying, "I require all their surplus property to be put into the hands of the bishop of my church in Zion."[3] And they will again be instructed that

...*Inasmuch as they receive more than is needful for their necessities and their wants, it shall be given into my storehouse;*

And the benefits shall be consecrated unto the inhabitants of Zion, and unto their generations, inasmuch as they become heirs according to the laws of the kingdom.

Behold, *this is what the Lord requires of every man in his steward-ship,* even as I, the Lord, have appointed *or shall hereafter appoint* unto any man.

And behold, *none are exempt from this law who belong to the church of the living God.*[4]

They can anticipate the instruction that

...Zion must arise and put on her beautiful garments.

Therefore I give unto you this commandment, that ye *bind yourselves by this covenant,* and it shall be done according to the laws of the land.

Behold, here is wisdom also in me for your good.

And you are to be equal, or in other words, *you are to have equal claims on the properties,* for the benefit of managing the concerns of your stewardships, *every man according to his wants and his needs, in-asmuch as his wants are just—*

And all this *for the benefit of the church of the living God, that every man may improve upon his talent, that every man may gain other talents,* yea, even an hundred fold, to be cast into the Lord's storehouse, to become the common property of the whole church—[5]

---

1. D & C 78:13-14.
2. D & C 104:15-16.
3. D & C 119:1.

4. D & C 70:7-10.
5. D & C 82:14-18.

The Lord has stressed the attitude with which the saints must function when the principles of the united order are restored, emphasizing that every man must be "seeking the interest of his neighbor, and doing all things with an eye single to the glory of God,"[1] and warning that "in your temporal things you shall be equal, *and this not grudgingly*, otherwise the abundance of the manifestations of the Spirit shall be withheld."[2]

When this eternal principle[3] is restored, the Lord has warned of severe penalties which will come upon those who harden their hearts against it. His instruction is that they "shall be dealt with according to the laws of my church, and shall be delivered over to the buffetings of Satan until the day of redemption."[4] The person who breaks the covenant of the united order, according to the Lord, "shall be cursed in his life, and shall be trodden down by whom I will,"[5] and shall eventually "lift up his eyes in hell, being in torment."[6] Those who won't abide by the law of the united order in the days of the New Jerusalem "shall not be found worthy to abide among you."[7]

Thus a vital aspect of the spiritual preparation of the saints is that they condition themselves to the future acceptance of the principles of the united order. Their willingness to share for the common good may hold the key to both spiritual and temporal salvation in the days to come.

21. Resolve to attain eternal goals: Endure to the end. Much has been written about the judgments God will pour out in the last days. Comment has been made about the testing of the saints, and concerning the possibility of the saints receiving chastening from the Almighty. It appears that there will be many trials to be endured, and that the future will not be easy. In the face of such a possibility, it is imperative that the Lord's people fix their sights clearly upon the attaining of their eternal goals. They must commit to themselves, to their families, and to their Father in Heaven that no matter what comes, they will endure to the end, overcoming their trials and obstacles. They will set a course to obtain their

---

1. D & C 82:19.
2. D & C 70:14.
3. See D & C 82:20; 104:1; 119:4.
4. D & C 82:21. See 104:9.
5. D & C 104:5. See verses 2-9; 105:6.
6. D & C 104:18.
7. D & C 119:5. See also verse 6.

salvation and exaltation, and not be swayed from it by the trials of the last days.

The Lord has promised that *"if you keep my commandments and endure to the end you shall have eternal life,* which gift is the greatest of all the gifts of God."[1]

He has warned of the condemnation that will await the fearful and unbelieving,[2] while promising that *"he that endureth in faith and doeth my will, the same shall overcome,* and shall receive an inheritance upon the earth when the day of transfiguration shall come."[3]

"The Lord giveth no commandments unto the children of men, save *he shall prepare a way for them* that they may accomplish the thing which he commandeth them."[4] The Father has given the saints *"power to overcome all things* which are not ordained of him—"[5] The saints have been instructed to "pray continually, that ye may not be tempted above that which ye can bear."[6] There is power granted to every man, then, to fulfill the commandments, overcome the challenges and resist the temptations which may come.

The hardships may become intense. The saints may have to "endure" in the fullest sense of the word. They may cry out in sorrow, as did the prophet Alma, "How long shall we suffer these great afflictions, O Lord? O Lord, give us strength according to our faith which is in Christ, even unto deliverance."[7] They may feel God has abandoned them, and cry out to him in anguish, as did the prophet Joseph:

> O God, where art thou? And where is the pavilion that covereth thy hiding place?
> How long shall thy hand be stayed, and thine eye, yea thy pure eye, behold from the eternal heavens the wrongs of thy people and of thy servants, and thine ear be penetrated with their cries?
> Yea, O Lord, how long shall they suffer these wrongs and unlawful oppressions, before thine heart shall be softened toward them, and thy bowels be moved with compassion toward them?[8]

Yet the eternal goal cannot be abandoned, and "blessed are they who are faithful and endure, whether in life or in death, for they shall inherit eternal life."[9] They must be like the Lamanite

---

1. D & C 14:7.
2. D & C 63:17-18.
3. D & C 63:20.
4. 1 Ne. 3:7. See 1 Ne. 17:3, 50-51.
5. D & C 50:35.
6. Al. 13:28.
7. Al. 14:26.
8. D & C 121:1-3.
9. D & C 50:5.

converts of old: "They never did look upon death with any degree of terror, for their hope and views of Christ and the resurrection; therefore, *death was swallowed up to them by the victory of Christ over it.*"[1] And they must be like the missionaries who labored in Book of Mormon times, whose afflictions "were swallowed up in the joy of Christ."[2] As one prophet expressed his confidence in prayer, *"I will cry unto thee in all mine afflictions, for in thee is my joy."*[3]

Yes, the saints would do well to fix their path upon the eternal goal, and resolve that they will endure to the end, no matter what trials they must overcome.

Temporal Preparations for Survival

22. Anticipate physical needs: Store food, clothing, fuel. The saints have been counseled repeatedly to store the supplies needed to preserve life in times of shortage and want. Theirs is the responsibility to prepare for their own personal and family needs, and also to anticipate the needs of many who will gather together in times of future distress. As Heber C. Kimball explained, *"This is a part of our religion—to lay up stores and provide for ourselves and for the surrounding country;* for the day is near when they will come by thousands and by millions, with their fineries, to get a little bread."[4]

Many events can cause shortages and scarcity of necessary commodities. Besides the obvious dangers of crop failure and war, consider other possibilities: strikes, transportation breakdown, economic upheaval, energy shortages, disruption of farming, quarantine against pestilence, etc. The supply of basic commodities is directly dependent upon manpower, equipment, and profit. If it becomes unprofitable to manufacture, distribute, or sell commodities, the items will either disappear from the stores or exorbitantly increase in price until the average family cannot afford to purchase them.

Serious difficulties can develop overnight. Food stores were suddenly left bare in many parts of the nation, for instance, as the "Cuban crisis" developed. The "great depression" erupted in a matter of hours as the stock market collapsed. The "energy crisis"

1. Al. 27:28.

2. Al. 31:38.

3. Al. 33:11.

4. *JD* 5:163-164. August 30, 1857.

emerged abruptly, with no meaningful advance warning to the general public.

Because of the possibility of rapid changes, and because of the prophetic warnings of future hardships, it is vital that an effective preparedness program be established in every family unit.

Several brief suggestions might prove helpful:

A.   *Anticipate emergency situations.* Think what would happen in a variety of situations such as a prolonged power failure, an extended transportation strike which would leave stores bare, a major disaster such as an earthquake, etc. What would you need if you were unable to buy anything from local merchants? Record your observations and analyze them in terms of preparatory actions required.

B.   *Inventory present needs and supplies.* No meaningful storage program can be developed without proper assessment of needs and the setting of realistic goals and timetables. No comprehensive, long-range storage program can be maintained without a record-keeping system. The inventory should include food, clothing, fuel, and household necessities. Anticipate family growth and needs for years to come.

C.   *Store medical and sanitation supplies.* If severe shortages occurred, people would soon feel particular need for basic medicinal goods to ward off the typical minor ailments with which families are beset. There would also be need for disinfectants, first aid supplies, home pesticides, etc.

D.   *Buy home maintenance supplies.* If difficult times come, there is a definite possibility of extended periods in which basic services such as power and fuel supply are maintained, but in which many necessary items are unavailable from merchants. There is wisdom in storing a basic supply of nuts and bolts, nails, faucet washers, toilet parts, electrical switches, light bulbs, etc. Every home should have basic tools for repair and construction available.

E.   *Involve the neighborhood in storage activities.* Latter-day Saints have been commanded to warn their neighbors and to prepare them for coming judgments.[1] In no situation is this command more imperative than in the area of storage of survival commodities. In a time of real shortage, unprepared neighbors could cause serious dilemmas of both a moral and temporal nature.

F.   *Avoid the "hoarding" mentality.* In times of scarcity, the "have nots" tend to accuse the "haves" of hoarding. The pub-

---

1. D & C 88:81, 84.

licity they generate can sometimes place a viable storage program in an unfavorable light, causing discouragement and even persecution. Systematically-spaced buying, rather than "panic buying," tends to dispel this attitude. Prior emphasis and community publicity on the advantages of food storage and preparedness will help place the practice in better prospective.

G. *Plant a garden.* Prepare to be self-supporting to as great a degree as possible. Successful gardening requires skill and experience which cannot be learned overnight, and it often requires long-range soil development. Tools should be acquired. Seeds should be stored. Records should be kept.

H. *Obtain a survival library.* Many books explain helpful techniques for self-sufficient living. Building a basic library on food storage and preservation, gardening, home repair, and outdoor survival is a wise precaution.

I. *Provide emergency heating and cooling facilities.* Emergency ability to maintain warmth in even one room could be the means of averting severe discomfort and suffering in a fuel shortage or power outage. There should also be provision for emergency cooking on the stove or fireplace. A supply of wood or coal should be on hand. There should be some provision for the emergency refrigeration of foodstuffs in case of prolonged power failure.

J. *Insulate homes.* Advance effort to properly insulate homes would be of particular value in times of fuel shortages. Adding insulation, upgrading window quality, installing weather stripping and storm doors—all are effective preparedness measures as well as hedges against rapidly-rising fuel costs.

K. *Repair, paint homes.* A vital aspect of preparedness is having the home in good repair. Plumbing, heating, electrical items, the roof, exterior surfaces—every aspect of a home should be maintained in good condition. Homes should be painted. Once hard times come, it is difficult to meet the costs of such repairs.

L. *Replace worn appliances.* Old stoves, refrigerators, toilets, and other necessary appliances should be upgraded while supplies are plentiful.

M. *Provide for home security from theft.* Scarcity of food and other necessary supplies would cause a serious increase in the danger of theft. Preparation should be made to maintain the security of the home.

N. *Safe storage of important records.* In the event of major disruptions or emergencies, there might be increased need for ready access to vital family records. Such records should be cataloged and preserved in a safe place, protected from fire and water damage and from theft. There might also be a need for ready access to addresses of family members and other important directions for distant geographical areas.

O.   *Maintain mobility and travel potential.* In case of serious emergency, families might find it necessary to travel relatively long distances to reach shelter in the homes of other family members or acquaintances. An automobile should be maintained in good working order, and an adequate supply of gas should be safely stored in portable containers. An emergency travel kit should be planned and prepared. Maps should be on hand.

P.   *Pre-arranged emergency travel plan.* The chance of having to rapidly leave one area and travel to another increases as the possibility of future war increases. Contingency decisions should be made, and all family members should be made aware of them.

23. Anticipate the possibility of nuclear war: Strengthen civil defense. Numerous prophecies of the last days warn of the danger of a Third World War and clearly assert that such a conflict will come to pass.[1]   Current media reports frequently cite evidence of Russia's continuing increase in offensive weaponry, on a scale which indicates the intent of "aggressive action." Of particular concern are other news reports indicating Ameriaca's vulnerability to attack, which predict the probable destruction of over a third of the U.S. population should a sudden nuclear assault occur.

In the author's opinion, there is vital need to strengthen the nation's civil defense program, making greatly increased provision for protection from nuclear attack. The fallout shelter program should be re-emphasized, with renewed effort to locate new shelters, restock existing shelters, and inform and educate the public. It is the author's belief that thoughtful citizens should exert their influence at the local, the state, and the national level, calling for immediate action to strengthen the land against attack.

Much has been said about America's offensive capability, and there are those who monitor it closely. In the light of Russia's rapid increase in military might, it is imperative that a strong offensive force be maintained. But that offensive force will not prevent attack on America's homeland, nor preserve the people if an attack occurs. There is immediate need to strengthen the nation's defense capability as well as offensive capacity.

---

1. See *Inspired Prophetic Warnings*, pp. 182-240, and *Prophecy—Key To The Future*, pp. 10-15.

On an individual level, it would be wise for families to carefully consider the need for a family fallout shelter. With many federal shelters now unstocked, citizens are increasingly vulnerable and often have no alternative but to make personal provision for protection against fallout. They need to re-educate themselves concerning the dangers of nuclear radiation, and discover that a two-week shelter stay would be far less than adequate protection against radiation sickness if one of Russia's huge new warheads were exploded nearby, with its larger radiation output and resulting extended period of radioactive decay.

Remember, the warning of prophecy is that a Third World War will occur, and that it will include the bombing of America's homeland, with severe loss resulting.

24. Anticipate the danger of economic upheaval: Be free from debt. As the world enters the trauma of the last days, economic stability may become increasingly fragile. Shortages of supplies may occur. Production may cease. Transportation and distribution systems may become inoperative. There continues to be the dual dangers of inflation and depression. War always influences the economy.

With the potential for economic instability looming ever more ominous as perilous times approach, there is wisdom in proceeding cautiously in matters of personal finance. These suggestions are offered:

A. *Be free from debt.* This counsel has been given to Latter-day Saints by their leaders on many occasions. It is wise instruction. In times of difficulty, indebtedness becomes financial bondage, and those who are in debt are not in full control of either their lives or their property. Set a course which will repay all indebtedness as soon as possible. That may not be the most profitable course for "good" times, but the freedom and security it offers for troubled times far outweighs the profit lost.

B. *Place preparation for security before pleasure and profit.* In establishing personal priorities, recognize the value of proper food storage, home care, and other basics of personal security over the many luxury items which are available. Preparation for future family well-being should take precedence over boats, campers, and speculative financial ventures.

C. *Be self-sustaining.* Every effort should be made for able-bodied individuals to provide for their own needs, and to resist the temptation to draw from government welfare programs. Those who do not provide for their own needs are not free, and are locked into unproductive situations which will not allow them to make adequate preparations for the future, nor enjoy life fully in the present. There is no effective substitute for personal effort and the development of individual skills and abilities.

D.   *Provide for financial emergencies.* A family needs a cushion of readily-available capital to serve as protection against sudden emergencies. An amount equal to six month's income is often recommended. There is also need for the protection available through insurance programs.

E.   *Recognize that money has value only in a working economy.* Money is only a means of exchange and has no value in and of itself. It can be used to obtain goods and services in normal times, but may be worthless in times of economic distress. There is wisdom in obtaining needed and desired items before periods of instability arise.

24. Anticipate communication disruption: Make long range emergency plans. Communication and transportation networks could be seriously disrupted or destroyed in the event of war or internal strife. Many of today's families are scattered across the nation. There is wisdom in establishing a family emergency plan, specifying what steps the family would take to be reunited or maintain family ties in the event of major problems in the nation, fixing dates and places for future meetings, proposing alternate communication systems, etc. A formal family organization would strengthen the emergency plans.

Interacting with Others in the Last Days Environment

The duties of the American citizen are many, and require diligent service and loyalty to the principles of freedom if liberty is to be preserved. A present role of the saints is to be a stabilizing influence in the many communities in which they reside across the land.

25. Fulfill the responsibilities of citizenship: Obey the laws of the land. As the perilous days of the "Saturday night of time" draw closer, it is vital that obedience be rendered to the laws of the land and that governmental stability be maintained. The Lord has revealed his counsel on this matter, instructing his people to

Let no man break the laws of the land, for *he that keepeth the laws of God hath no need to break the laws of the land.*

Wherefore, *be subject to the powers that be*, until he reigns whose right it is to reign, and subdues all enemies under his feet.[1]

He has commanded the saints to support laws which maintain man's freedom, rights and privileges:

...Verily I say unto you concerning the laws of the land, it is my will that my people should observe to do all things whatever I command them.

And that law of the land which is constitutional, supporting that principle of freedom in maintaining rights and privileges, belongs to all mankind, and is justifiable before me.

Therefore, I, the Lord, justify you, and your brethren of my church, in befriending that law which is the constitutional law of the land;

And as pertaining to law of man, whatever is more or less than this, cometh of evil.

I, the Lord God, make you free, therefore ye are free indeed, and the law also maketh you free.[2]

A declaration of belief regarding governments and laws was adopted by the Church in 1835, which asserts that "we believe that governments were instituted of God for the benefit of man; and that he holds men accountable for their acts in relation to them,...."[3] That declaration holds that governments should make and administer laws "for the good and safety of society,"[4] and that governments are to frame and hold inviolate laws which accomplish three purposes:

1. secure to each individual the free exercise of conscience,[5]
2. secure to each individual the right and control of property, and
3. secure to each individual the protection of life.[6]

That declaration also holds that "*to the laws all men owe respect and deference, as without them peace and harmony would*

---

1. D & C 58:21-22.
2. D & C 98:4-8.
3. D & C 134:1.
4. *Ibid.*
5. Note that the Lord said this was his purpose in establishing the U.S. Constitution, "That every man may act in doctrine and principle pertaining to futurity, *according to the moral agency which I have given unto him, that every man may be accountable for his own sins in the day of judgment.*" (D & C 101:78. See verses 79-80.)
6. D & C 134:2.

be supplanted by anarchy and terror;..."[1] Such a period of anarchy, or internal conflict, is clearly indicated by many prophetic warnings concerning America's future.[2] It appears obvious that anarchy will be averted, in that future period, only to the degree that America's citizens maintain peace and stability through obedience to law and loyal allegiance to existing governments.

What can each individual do to support his country and render obedience to the laws of the land? The author listed the following suggestions in the program to a patriotic bicentennial pageant which he wrote and directed. They were presented under the title, "What Can *I* Do To Preserve My Freedoms?"

1.   I'll study the Constitution and the basic documents of America with my family.

2.   I'll fly the flag, and respect it as the symbol of our country.

3.   I'll make national holidays a special time to teach my children their national heritage.

4.   I'll pledge to keep myself and my family free from sin and the evils of the land.

5.   I'll have respect for law and order, and for those who administer the law.

6.   I'll know what my children are studying in school, and encourage school officials to promote patriotism and loyalty.

7.   I'll work to keep our community and country clean and beautiful.

8.   I'll do an honest day's work, and be honest and above reproach in all my dealings.

9.   I'll study the scriptures and know the prophetic promises and warnings revealed concerning this great land.

10.   I'll teach my children the value of work, and strengthen their qualities of self-reliance and personal initiative.

11.   I'll support clubs and organizations which are working to build character and establish positive values.

12.   I'll actively resist crime and corruption, and be alert to dangers such as vandalism, drugs, and pornography.

13.   I'll strengthen my family relationships and make my family unit a solid building block of society.

14.   I'll prepare for the possibility of difficult times ahead by having an emergency supply of food and clothing and being free from debt.

---

1. D & C 134:6.
2. See also *Prophecy—Key to the Future*, pp. 40-66.

15.   I'll speak out for what I believe, but be sure my statements are characterized by dignity, decency, maturity of thought, and knowledge of the facts.

16.   I'll study and properly prepare myself for a vocation so

17.   I'll be aware of the rising strength of potential enemies to our freedom, and be alert to changes in the international balance of power.

18.   I'll work to help good men be elected, and seek to have governmental officials accountable for their actions.

19.   I'll read and learn what actually happens when people fall into bondage, so I can understand the freedoms we sometimes take for granted.

20.   I'll know the political candidates who can shape my way of life, and support only those I feel will serve competently and righteously.

21.   I'll support programs and policies which make government the servant of the people, rather than people the servants of government.

22.   I'll study the effects of opposing ideologies on our peace and liberty so I can recognize these theories and those who teach them.

23.   I'll list the principles and policies which I believe will help preserve our freedom, and then work to support them.

24.   I'll subscribe to a patriotic publication and try to be well-informed on current events.

25.   I'll study the major local, state, and national political issues, and know where I stand concerning them.

26.   I'll be aware of our national defense capabilities, and work to keep my country prepared.

27.   I'll obey the scriptural commandments to warn others of the judgments that are coming if the people of this nation allow wickedness to prevail.

28.   I'll preach the gospel by word and by example, for I know that the righteousness of the people is the key to this nation's destiny.

29.   I'll pray each day for our country and for its leaders, asking God to let His blessings and protection continue with us.[1]

---

1. Program, *This Is My Country*, presented by the Bountiful, Utah Stake, March 12 and 13, 1976, in the Bountiful Regional Center.

26. **Elect good leaders: Uphold honest and wise men.** In this era when the nation has plunged rapidly towards wickedness which may bring God's judgments, it is essential that the tide be stemmed, by choosing men of integrity for positions of governmental leadership. God has revealed that

> ...*When the wicked rule the people mourn.*
> Wherefore, honest men and wise men should be sought for diligently, and good men and wise men ye should observe to uphold; otherwise whatsoever is less than these cometh of evil. [1]

The declaration of belief regarding governments and laws states that

> We believe that all governments necessarily require civil officers and magistrates to enforce the laws of the same; and that *such as will administer the law in equity and justice should be sought for and upheld* by the voice of the people if a republic, or the will of the sovereign. [2]

Latter-day Saints believe they should work within the governmental system to accomplish necessary ends. Criminals should be "delivered up and dealt with according to the laws of the land."[3] Those who have been wronged should "importune for redress, and redemption, by the hands of those who are placed as rulers and are in authority over you—according to the laws and constitution of the people,..."[4] The saints are to be tolerant of others, and even of imperfections in the actions of their elected leaders, remembering the Lord's counsel:

> ...Verily I say unto you, and this is wisdom, make unto yourselves friends with the mammon of unrighteousness and they will not destroy you.
> *Leave judgment alone with me,* for it is mine and I will repay. [5]

27. **Prepare for future persecutions: Learn how to deal with enemies.** Another major message of prophecy is that the saints must endure severe persecution in a time yet future. The Lord has seen fit to give very specific instructions concerning how the saints should deal with those who oppose them. His people should be aware of these instructions and be prepared to abide by them if the need arises. He has told them to

---

1. D & C 98:9-11.
2. D & C 134:3.
3. D & C 42:79. See verses 84-86.

4. D & C 101:76-77. See verses 81-92.
5. D & C 82:22-23. See 58:20.

...Organize yourselves according to the laws of man; That your enemies may not have power over you; that you may be preserved in all things; that you may be enabled to keep my laws; that every bond may be broken wherewith the enemy seeketh to destroy my people.[1]

Revealed counsel has been given to "Be patient in afflictions, *revile not against those that revile.* Govern your house in meekness, and be steadfast."[2] The Lord has also commanded, "Behold, it is said in my laws, or forbidden, to get in debt to thine enemies."

Zion's Camp was taught other principles to help them be safe from their enemies. The Lord instructed them to "Talk not of judgments, neither boast of faith nor of mighty works, but *carefully gather together,* as much in one region as can be, consistently with the feelings of the people;..."[3] They were also told to

...Sue for peace, not only to the people that have smitten you, but also to all people:

And lift up an ensign of peace, and make a proclamation of peace unto the ends of the earth;

And make proposals for peace unto those who have smitten you, according to the voice of the Spirit which is in you, and all things shall work together for your good.[4]

While he was a prisoner in Liberty Jail, the prophet Joseph Smith set forth the duties of the saints in relation to their persecutors. He said it was their "imperative duty" to

1.   Be sure all the saints were informed and given knowledge of the sufferings and abuses which had been endured.[5]

2.   Be sure a record was kept of all damages sustained, both of character, personal injuries, and real property.[6]

3.   Be sure a record was kept of the names of all persons involved in instances of oppression.[7]

4.   Be sure to obtain evidence in the form of statements and affidavits.[8]

5.   Be sure to gather copies of all libelous publications.[9]

6.   Publish the above to all the world and present them to heads of government.[10]

---

1. D & C 44:4-5.
2. D & C 31:9.
3. D & C 105:24.
4. D & C 105:38-40.
5. D & C 123:1.

6. D & C 123:2.
7. D & C 123:3.
8. D & C 123:4.
9. D & C 123:4-5.
10. D & C 123:6.

All of the preceding is

> ...Enjoined on us by our Heavenly Father, before we can fully and completely claim that promise which shall call him forth from his hiding place; and also that *the whole nation may be left without excuse before he can send forth the power of his mighty arm.*[1]

Doctrine and Covenants section 98 contains a comprehensive explanation of how to deal with enemies who persecute the saints. The Lord has said,

> Now, I speak unto you concerning your families—*if men will smite you, or your families, once,* and ye bear it patiently and revile not against them, neither seek revenge, ye shall be rewarded;
> But if ye bear it not patiently, it shall be accounted unto you as being meted out as a just measure unto you.
> And again, *if your enemy shall smite you the second time,* and you revile not against your enemy, and bear it patiently, your reward shall be an hundred-fold.
> And again, *if he shall smite you the third time,* and ye bear it patiently, your reward shall be doubled unto you four-fold;
> *And these three testimonies shall stand against your enemy if he repent not, and shall not be blotted out.*
> And now, verily I say unto you, if that enemy shall escape my vengeance, that he be not brought into judgment before me, then *ye shall see to it that ye warn him in my name, that he come no more upon you, neither upon your family,* even your children's children unto the third and fourth generation.
> And then, if he shall come upon you or your children, or your children's children unto the third and fourth generation, *I have delivered thine enemy into thine hands;*
> And then if thou wilt spare him, thou shalt be rewarded for thy righteousness; and also thy children and thy children's children unto the third and fourth generation.
> *Nevertheless, thine enemy is in thine hands;* and if thou rewardest him according to his works thou art justified; *if he has sought thy life, and thy life is endangered by him, thine enemy is in thine hands and thou art justified.*[2]

The declaration of belief regarding governments and laws states that

> *We believe that men should appeal to the civil law for redress of all wrongs and grievances,* where personal abuse is inflicted or the right of

---

1. *Ibid.* He added that "there is much which lieth in futurity, pertaining to the saints, which depends upon these things." (D & C 123:15.)
2. D & C 98:23-31.

property or character infringed, where such laws exist as will protect the same; but we believe that *all men are justified in defending themselves, their friends, and property, and the government, from the unlawful assaults and encroachments of all persons in times of exigency,* where immediate appeal cannot be made to the laws, and relief afforded.[1]

Two passages from the Book of Mormon explain the motives under which it is appropriate to engage in combat with enemies. The first deals with the Nephites as they united to resist the Lamanites who were attacking under the leadership of their wicked chief captain, Zerahemnah:

> Nevertheless, the Nephites were inspired by a better cause, for *they were not fighting for monarchy nor power but they were fighting for their homes and their liberties, their wives and their children, and their all, yea, for their rites of worship and their church.*
>
> And they were doing that which they felt was the *duty which they owed to their God;* for the Lord had said unto them, and also unto their fathers, that: *Inasmuch as ye are not guilty of the first offense, neither the second, ye shall not suffer yourselves to be slain by the hands of your enemies.*
>
> And again, the Lord has said that: *Ye shall defend your families even unto bloodshed.* Therefore for this cause were the Nephites contending with the Lamanites, *to defend themselves, and their families, and their lands, their country, and their rights, and their religion.*[2]

The second describes the motives of the Nephites as they united under the leadership of General Moroni:

> *Now the Nephites were taught to defend themselves against their enemies, even to the shedding of blood if it were necessary;* yea, and they were also taught *never to give an offense,* yea, and *never to raise the sword except it were against an enemy, except it were to preserve their lives.*
>
> And this was their faith, that by so doing God would prosper them in the land, or in other words, if they were faithful in keeping the commandments of God that *he would prosper them in the land; yea, warn them to flee, or to prepare for war, according to their danger;*
>
> And also, that *God would make it known unto them whither they should go to defend themselves against their enemies,* and by so doing, the Lord would deliver them; and this was the faith of Moroni, and his heart did glory in it; not in the shedding of blood but *in doing good, in preserving his people, yea, in keeping the commandments of God, yea, and resisting iniquity.*[3]

---

1. D & C 134:11.
2. Al. 43:45-47.

3. Al. 48:14-16.

If enemies attempt to drive the saints from the land of Zion,[1] the Lord has instructed his people that

> ...Ye shall curse them;
> And whomsoever ye curse, I will curse and ye shall avenge me of mine enemies.
> And my presence shall be with you even in avenging me of mine enemies, unto the third and fourth generation of them that hate me.[2]

During all the events of the future, the saints should remember the Lord's decree that they will prevail against their enemies so long as they keep his commandments:

> Behold, they shall, for I have decreed it, begin to prevail against mine enemies from this very hour.
> And by hearkening to observe all the words which I, the Lord their God, shall speak unto them, they shall never cease to prevail until the kingdoms of the world are subdued under my feet, and the earth is given unto the saints, to possess it forever and ever.
> But inasmuch as they keep not my commandments, and hearken not to observe all my words, the kingdoms of the world shall prevail against them.[3]

In Conclusion

Thus ends this account of God's message concerning the events of the last days. It is scriptural. It is accurate in its interpretation. It is true. It is written in partial fulfillment of the inspired prayer of Joseph Smith, in which he asked the Savior to

> Put upon thy servants the testimony of the covenant, that when they go out and proclaim thy word they may seal up the law, and prepare the hearts of thy saints for all those judgments thou art about to send, in thy wrath, upon the earth, because of their transgressions, that thy people may not faint in the day of trouble.[4]

---

1. See D & C 64:41-43; 45:66-75.
2. D & C 103:24-26. See verses 2-3. This commandment differs from the Savior's instruction to "love your enemies" (see Mt. 5:38-45), but is in accordance with other passages of scripture: Al. 33:10; D & C 109: 50-53; 133:40, 42-43. It conforms to the Lord's commandment that the saints should leave a witness against the wicked in the last days. (See pp. 79-82)
3. D & C 103:6-8.
4. D & C 109:38.

It has not been an easy book to write. Neither has it been a pleasant one, for it speaks of tragic events which will bring much sorrow and suffering upon the land and people I love. But the Spirit gave repeated instruction that it come forth, and I have sought to obey. If it were in my power to turn away the prophesied calamities, I would do so, and save the nation from the impending judgments. I recognize that deliverance will only be granted to the Lord's people who live in righteousness, and I seek to be numbered among them. My sentiments were well expressed in the prayer of dedication offered by the prophet Joseph:

> O Lord, *we delight not in the destruction of our fellow man;* their souls are precious before thee;
> *But thy word must be fulfilled.* Help thy servants to say, with thy grace assisting them: Thy will be done, O Lord, and not ours.
> We know that thou hast spoken by the mouth of thy prophets *terrible things concerning the wicked, in the last days—that thou wilt pour out thy judgments, without measure;*
> Therefore, O Lord, *deliver thy people from the calamity of the wicked;* enable thy servants to seal up the law, and bind up the testimony, that they may be prepared against the day of burning.[1]

Ye saints, remember that "All victory and glory is brought to pass unto you through your diligence, faithfulness, and prayers of faith."[2] Put on the whole armor of God, "That ye may be able to withstand the evil day,"[3] and look forward to the day when the Church will arise and "Shine forth fair as the moon, clear as the sun, and terrible as an army with banners; and be adorned as a bride...."[4] "Fear not to do good,"[5] and trust in the Lord as he brings about the establishment of his Zion and prepares the pure in heart. Find joy in the anticipation of his peaceable kingdom, and remember that he has instructed the saints to

> ...Let your hearts be comforted concerning Zion; for all flesh is in mine hands; *be still and know that I am God.*[6]

Summary

1. This chapter has been written to assist those desiring to adopt an effective course for the future. It summarizes scriptural

---

1. D & C 109:43-46.
2. D & C 103:36.
3. D & C 27:15-18. See Eph. 6:10-17.

4. D & C 109:73-74.
5. D & C 6:33-34.
6. D & C 101:16.

counsel for proper attitudes and conduct, and attempts to point out a viable path that will safely lead through the perilous times to come.

2.   It is wise to adopt attitudes concerning the last days which are based on eternal perspective. Attempting to envision the events to come from God's point of view can help man to properly orient his life. Eight observations were made:

A.   God directs the affairs of man.
B.   God desires to bless and reward man.
C.   Last day's judgments are part of man's mortal probation.
D.   God chastens those he loves.
E.   Death is sweet to those who die in the Lord.
F.   There must be a transition to Christ's millennial kingdom.
G.   The earth is approaching the end of its temporal existence.
H.   Look forward to the blessings of the millennial era.

3.   Scriptural counsel was cited concerning spiritual preparations for survival. The saints have been instructed to

A.   Cleanse themselves from sins which bring judgments: Repent.
B.   Escape judgments through obedience: Keep God's commandments.
C.   Be free from the sins of the generation: Sanctify themselves.
D.   Prepare spiritually: Be guided by the Holy Ghost.
E.   Recognize last day's events: Watch for signs of the times.
F.   Teach doctrines of the last days: Seek knowledge for protection.
G.   Prepare the saints for the hour of judgment: Warn their neighbor.
H.   Preach repentance to non-members: Warn of coming judgments.
I.   Bind the law and seal the testimony: Testify against the wicked.
J.   Go ye out from Babylon: Be separate from the wicked.
K.   Seek divine strength, guidance and protection: Pray always.

    L.   Prepare for return of the united order: Be ready to share.

    M.   Resolve to attain eternal goals: Endure to the end.

4.   Temporal preparations for survival were also recommended, which included the following principles and instructions:

    A.   Anticipate physical needs: Store food, clothing, fuel.

    B.   Anticipate the reality of nuclear war: Strengthen civil defense.

    C.   Anticipate the danger of economic upheaval: Be free from debt.

    D.   Anticipate communication disruption: Make long-range emergency plans.

5.   Scriptural counsel for interacting with others in the last days was presented, together with many suggestions for being an effective citizen. This counsel was summarized under the following categories:

    A.   Fulfill the responsibilities of citizenship: Obey the laws of the land.

    B.   Elect good leaders: Uphold honest and wise men.

    C.   Prepare for future persecution: Learn how to deal with enemies.

6.   As the events of the last days unfold, the saints must be willing to say "Thy will be done, O Lord, and not ours," and then "be still and know" that God is governing the affairs of men.

List of Quotations

BOOK OF MORMON

1 Nephi

2:20	13
3:7	92
4:13-14	13
5:4-5	13
5:4-5	14
12:1	14
12:2	14
12:4-5	14
12:6-10	14
12:11-15	14
12:19-20	14
12:21	14
12:22-23	14
13:1-9	14
13:3	14
13:10	14
13:12	14
13:13	15
13:14	15
13:15-16	15
13:17-19	15
13:20-29	15
13:30	15
13:30-31	15
13:34-35	15
13:37	16
14:12	83
14:12	85

2 Nephi

1:5-7	16
2:21	63
9:27	63
10:10-11	16
10:19	17
33:9	63

Jacob

2:12	17

Mosiah

5:5-7	64
7:29, 33	87
9:3, 17-18	87
11:23-25	87
21:14-15	87

Alma

10:22-23	88
12:24	63
13:11-12	71
13:28	92
14:11	82
14:26	92
24:7-27	66
27:28	93
31:38	93
33:10	89
33:10	106
33:11	93
34:28	88
42:4	63
43:45-47	105
48:14-16	105

Helaman

3:35	71

3 Nephi

12:30	66
21:4	16

Mormon

2:13-15, 6:7	65

Ether

1:42-43	17
2:7	17
2:15	18
10:28	18
13:2-3	18
13:6-8	18

Moroni

10:32-33	71

PEARL OF GREAT PRICE

Moses

1:39	62
6:27	78
7:64	68

Articles of Faith

10	67

DOCTRINE & COVENANTS

1:8-9	81
1:9	69
1:12-13	77
1:33	70
5:18	80
6:33-34	107
10:46-52	88
10:49-51	19
11:12-14	73
14:7	92
14:8	73
19:4-5	69
19:15	69
20:17-18	62
24:15-17	81
24:19	80
27:15-18	107
29:8	85
29:11	67
29:26	67
29:42-44	63
31:4	80
31:8	77
31:8	83
31:9	103
33:2-4	80
33:10	77
33:10	78
34:6	80
34:6-10	79
35:16	74
35:24	71
38:1-3	62
38:8	71
38:11-12	80
38:18-22	19
38:22	66
38:22	68
38:28-31	76
38:29-31	19
38:40-41	78
39:16-18	88
41:1	62
41:4	66
42:36	85
42:44-47	66
42:79, 84-86	102
43:20-21	79
43:24-25	62
44:4-5	103
45:2,6	71
45:32	84
45:39,44	74
45:44	75
45:56-57	73
45:59	67
45:66	85
45:66-67	106
45:68-69	85
48:1	83
49:23	75
49:26-27	70
50:5	92
50:35	92
58:2-4	63
58:5	75
58:6	75
58:6	79
58:20	102
58:21-22	99
58:28	62
59:16-21	62
60:15	81
61:38	74
61:39	87
63:2-4, 49-51	66
63:17-18	92
63:20	92
63:24	84
63:32	80
63:36-37	79
63:37	85
63:50	68
63:63	70
63:64	73
64:41-43	106
65:1-3	77
68:10-11	74
68:11-12	81
70:7-10	90
70:14	91
75:18-22	81
76:5-6, 7-10	62
76:116	73

77:6	67	100:13	64	109:50-53	106	65:23	68
78:13-14	90	100:15	62	109:54	25	65:25	68
82:5-6	80	101:1-5	64	109:73-74	107		
82:14-18	90	101:5	62	111:11	62	*Joel*	
82:19	91	101:7	87	112:33	72	2:28	68
82:20	91	101:10-16	66	112:33-34	69		
82:21	91	101:16	107	115:6	84		
82:22-23	92	101:22	84	119:1	90	**NEW TESTAMENT**	
84:33	72	101:28	68	119:4	91	*Matthew*	
84:55-59	70	101:29	68	119:5,6	91	5:38-45	106
84:80-84	66	101:32	68	121:1-3	92	6:25-34	66
84:87	3	101:35-38	66	121:28	68	7:24-27	61
84:87	78	101:64-68	84	122:1-7	65	10:38-39	66
84:92-97	81	101:68	84	122:7-8	65	16:24-27	66
84:117	70	101:76-77,		123:1	103	23:37	63
85:3	77	81-92	102	123:2	103	24:14	80
87:6	69	101:77-80	25	123:3	103	24:32-33	74
87:8	84	101:78,		123:4	103	24:42	75
88:18-19	67	79-80	99	123:4-5	103	25:13	75
88:19-20	67	101:92	88	123:6	103		
88:25-26	67	103:4	64	123:15	104	*Mark*	
88:40	62	103:6-8	106	124:10	65	13:35-37	75
88:41	62	103:11-14	63	124:36	84		
88:63-65	73	103:24-26	81	124:93	81	*Luke*	
88:67-68	72	103:27-28	66	124:124	81	11:49-51	82
88:73-75,		103:36	107	128:8-11	81	12:37-40	75
85,138	72	104:1	89	130:2	68	21:34-36	75
88:77-80	76	104:1	91	131:5	81		
88:79	77	104:5	91	133:4	85	*John*	
88:81	3	104:2-9	91	133:4-5, 10,		14:26	73
88:81	77	104:9	91	19	77	15:26	73
88:81	91	104:15-16	90	133:5	82	16:13	73
88:84	81	104:2-3	106	133:25	67		
88:84-85	77	104:24-26	106	133:40,		*Romans*	
88:86	70	104:17	62	42-43	106	8:28	62
88:92	77	104:17	68	133:40, 42-43	89		
88:118	76	104:18	91	133:71-72	81	*Ephesians*	
88:126	87	105:1-10	89	134:1	99	6:10-17	107
90:24	62	105:4-5	89	134:2	99	6:18	75
95:1	8	105:6	91	134:3	102		
95:1	64	105:24	103	134:6	100	*I. Thessalonians*	
97:12-14	76	105:38-40	103	134:11	105	5:6	75
97:24-25	70	105:40	62	134:31	64		
98:4-8	99	106:4-5	75	136:32-33	73	*I. Peter*	
98:5-6	25	109:38	77	136:42	71	4:7	75
98:9-11	102	109:38	81				
98:11-13	71	109:38	106	**BIBLE**		*Revelation*	
98:14-15	63	109:42	72			7:3	72
98:21-22	70	109:43-46	107	**OLD TESTAMENT**		9:6	65
98:23-31	104	109:45-46	77	*Isaiah*		16:15	75
99:4-5	81	109:50-52	89	11:9	68	20:1-3	68